Self-Directed IRA Investing:
A BiggerPockets Guide

Self-Directed IRA Investing

A BiggerPockets Guide

with Kaaren Hall

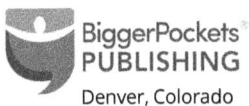

BiggerPockets
PUBLISHING
Denver, Colorado

Self-Directed IRA Investing: A BiggerPockets Guide
Kaaren Hall

Published by BiggerPockets Publishing LLC, Denver, CO
Copyright © 2025 by Kaaren Hall
All rights reserved.

Publisher's Cataloging-in-Publication Data
Names: Hall, Kaaren, author.
Title: Self-directed IRA investing : a BiggerPockets guide / Kaaren Hall.
Description: Denver, CO: BiggerPockets Publishing, LLC, 2025.
Identifiers: LCCN: 2024946853 | ISBN: 9781960178855 (paperback) | 9781960178862 (ebook)
Subjects: LCSH Self-directed individual retirement accounts. | Finance, Personal. | Investments. | Retirement income--Planning. | Financial security. | BISAC BUSINESS & ECONOMICS / Personal Finance / Retirement Planning | BUSINESS & ECONOMICS / Investments & Securities / Portfolio Management | BUSINESS & ECONOMICS / Personal Finance / Taxation
Classification: LCC HG179 .H35 2024 | DDC 332.024--dc23
LSI 10 9 8 7 6 5 4 3 2 1

BiggerPockets Guide
Mission Statement

Revolutionize your investing journey with BiggerPockets Guides: a series of laser-focused, in-depth strategy blueprints designed to help you master crucial real estate topics. These books tackle advanced investing subjects head-on, providing you with trustworthy insights that will supercharge your real estate journey.

Say goodbye to expensive guru courses and flashy masterminds: BiggerPockets Guides are your *affordable* ticket to real estate success. We've distilled the valuable knowledge of real experts into accessible guides that connect you with even more free tools and resources on the BiggerPockets site.

Whether you're a seasoned pro or just starting out, our guides will be your secret weapon in helping you navigate the lucrative world of real estate investing with confidence. Get ready to transform your financial future—one guide at a time!

Self-Directed Retirement Accounts and Your Retirement Future

What is one of the most pivotal, most powerful game changers for individuals who invest in real estate? It is the ability to take charge of their tax-protected investment accounts. Once you understand that you can choose how to invest your retirement funds, new doors open. Brighter golden years are possible. Once you realize Wall Street is not your only path—and in fact may not be the best, most effective path—you feel empowered.

Your new journey begins when you open a self-directed IRA, and this book will help you understand your options.

Self-directed individual retirement accounts (SDIRAs) offer a powerful tool for investors, asset sponsors, real estate professionals, and advisors to collaborate with a shared objective: winning in the real estate market. By understanding how SDIRAs operate, you can expand your retirement savings beyond Wall Street. For advisors, helping clients recognize the benefits of holding retirement funds in an SDIRA can greatly enhance the service they provide.

As an investor or real estate professional, grasping the advantages of SDIRAs is crucial. Once you do, remarkable opportunities arise. When executed effectively, SDIRA investments can transform neighborhoods and cities as investors and capital-raisers work together to revitalize communities. This growth not only improves the landscape but also creates more and better places to live and work. By self-directing your retirement funds into real estate, you may unlock new doors—both literally and figuratively—leading to increased profits and a more robust retirement nest egg.

While learning about SDIRAs, you are helping to create a better future for yourself and your loved ones. Imagine you open an SDIRA for your own investments and watch the proceeds grow tax free or tax deferred. You compound your retirement growth faster because the proceeds are not diminished by tax. Then you help others to do the same as they watch your success and want to mirror it.

The three main goals of self-directed IRA real estate investing are:

1. **Diversification beyond traditional assets**. By investing in real estate through an SDIRA, you can diversify your retirement portfolio beyond stocks and bonds, reducing risk and potentially increasing stability with tangible assets.

2. **Tax-advantaged growth**. SDIRAs offer the opportunity to grow your real estate investments tax free or tax deferred, depending on whether you use a Roth or Traditional IRA. This can lead to significant savings over time, as profits from real estate appreciation, rent, or sales can compound without immediate tax liabilities.

3. **Greater control over investments**. SDIRAs provide you with direct control over your investment choices. You can select specific properties or real estate ventures that align with your financial goals, giving you more influence over your retirement growth strategy.

If any of these goals resonate with you, then this guide is exactly what you need. Keep reading!

Prepare to Discover...

The power-packed financial advantages of self-directed individual retirement accounts (SDIRAs).

Here's what you'll learn:

- How SDIRAs work for real estate investors
- The size of the potential market
- What asset classes (in addition to real estate) are available
- How to put an action plan into play to boost your financial future
- How to leverage UDFI tax strategies and use debt with your SDIRA
- The role of due diligence when investing in real estate with an SDIRA
- How to maximize tax benefits and avoid penalties with SDIRAs and solo 401(k)s
- Success stories that demonstrate the potential of SDIRAs in real estate investments

Table of Contents

A Note from the Expert:

Welcome to the World
of SDIRAs

Oh, the self-directed IRA . . . one of the most powerful tools and best-kept secrets that few real estate investors (and average Joes) know about. The truth is that self-directed IRAs (SDIRAs) have been around for fifty years and have only recently seen a rise in popularity. This change stems from the latest financial recession, when people had to find another way to fund deals and grow their wealth rather than going through their local banks. As people will do, they found another way. Even today not enough people know about opening an SDIRA and why they should if they really want to reach their financial and retirement goals.

In what has become a $40 trillion pool of retirement assets, SDIRAs open up more avenues for people to use for their funding needs. The savvy investor today knows the value of investing in non-correlated assets. In simple terms, that is using one's SDIRA to invest in real estate and other holdings.

The good news is that the process is easier than you think.

Anyone can self-direct an IRA. There is no one type of individual who opens an SDIRA. The difference between an SDIRA and a traditional, third-party-managed retirement account is who holds the reins—who gets to make the decisions regarding where the retirement funds are invested. If a third party makes the decisions, your retirement funds can be placed in volatile stocks. Do you want a more stable outcome? Take the reins and make the decisions. As we say in the industry, "Invest in what you know best!" Your retirement funds can be used to invest in an array of financial vehicles.

If you are serious about building out retirement portfolios and saving and investing, an SDIRA may well be the answer. Want to invest in real estate, private stock, metals, or other alternative assets? Want to accelerate savings and have an investment vehicle that beats the stock market? Again, keep reading. Educate yourself so you can grow your retirement wealth, starting with opening an SDIRA and investing in what you know best.

As you embark on this journey into the world of self-directed retirement investing, I want to assure you that you're in capable hands. With nearly twenty years of experience in the self-directed retirement space, I've dedicated my career to helping individuals take control of their retirement savings and explore investment opportunities beyond traditional avenues. My extensive professional background, combined with my role as the founder/CEO of uDirect IRA Services, LLC equips me with the knowledge and expertise needed to guide you through this complex yet rewarding landscape.

The information in this book is drawn from reliable and authoritative sources, including www.IRS.gov and the Internal Revenue Code. These resources, coupled with my years of hands-on experience, ensure that you receive accurate, up-to-date, and practical advice. My goal is to demystify the complexities of SDIRAs, helping you to understand the rules, regulations, and opportunities that can significantly impact your financial future.

For the BiggerPockets community, this content is tailored to empower you to make informed decisions about your retirement investments. Whether you're a seasoned investor or just starting out, the insights and strategies shared in this book will help you leverage self-directed retirement accounts to build wealth, diversify your portfolio, and secure your financial future. I'm excited to share this knowledge with you and help you unlock the full potential of your retirement savings.

By the time you finish reading this guide, you will have a greater understanding of SDIRAs and the reasons why more people should open one.

If you have questions, please reach out to me via email, social media, through my website, or by calling my office. My staff and I stand by to answer your questions. We are happy to help.

Enjoy the book!

Kaaren Hall

Chapter 1

IRAs and Real Estate—An Overview

"It's the best-kept secret. And its growing popularity has grown because SDIRAs do provide access to capital."

How do individual retirement accounts (IRAs) and real estate overlap and complement each other?

The level of success that real estate investors can achieve is becoming increasingly intertwined with the use of SDIRAs. Investing in real estate is a growing trend. Awareness about the ability to self-direct retirement accounts as a vehicle for investing in real estate is also growing—but not quickly enough.

What Is a Self-Directed IRA?

Simply, an SDIRA enables individuals to choose where they want their funds invested. This gives the account owner the ability to invest in a variety of asset classes, including various methods of direct investment in real estate. No more leaving your financial future up to some unknown broker or fund manager and their commission-incentivized picks. You can choose where to invest. As an investor, you're all about strategy. You take the time to dive deep into the market, analyze trends, and make informed decisions to reach your investment goals. By doing this, you also benefit from the same great tax advantages typically associated with a 401(k) or a traditional IRA.

Who Can Use Self-Directed Retirement Accounts?

Every American can take advantage of these tax-saving investment tools. All you need is "active income" to make a contribution. Whether you are self-employed or a salaried wage earner (or if you inherited an IRA), you can use this tool.

To an individual, a couple, or a business owner, the SDIRA can be a tremendous tool for growing wealth, keeping more earnings, multiplying each dollar, and saving big on taxes. The SDIRA creates a way to snowball wealth and increase income gains in a way that puts the decision-making in the hands of the IRA owner.

The Relationship between IRAs and Real Estate Pros

Among a variety of other asset classes, SDIRAs can be used to invest in a wide range of opportunities beyond traditional stocks and bonds. While awareness of this investment strategy is growing, educating and empowering individuals to utilize it often depends on the financial advisors, investment consultants, or wealth managers they engage with. As an investor, it's crucial to seek out experienced professionals who can guide you through the complexities of self-directed investing and help you execute your strategy effectively.

SDIRAs are a powerful tool for you because they allow for direct investments in various property types, including single-family homes, condos, townhomes, and even commercial properties. These properties can be held within the IRA and rented out to generate steady (tax-free or tax-deferred) income in retirement, thus providing a unique opportunity to build wealth and diversify retirement portfolios through tangible assets.

You Owe it to Yourself

If you truly want to have the best possible experience with the best tools in the industry, you owe it to yourself to get educated. Learn and understand the benefits of the SDIRA. Understand the potential to make more on every real estate deal you make. Plus, with a better understanding of the SDIRA landscape, you can reduce your risk and ultimately have more capital to reinvest.

The additional gains are the result of the tax-free or tax-deferred nature of the retirement account. Those untaxed proceeds can go out into other investments and continue to compound.

By leveraging the benefits of SDIRAs, you can maximize your returns on investment properties, setting yourself apart as a knowledgeable and resourceful investor.

You also have . . .

- ✓ The satisfaction of knowing you're getting the most bang for the buck for yourself and for your future.
- ✓ The possibility of additional capital streams to invest in more and bigger deals each year.

✓ The ability to teach your friends and family what you learn so they can also grow their retirement future.

✓ A tactic you can put on rinse and repeat—then scale.

The Caveat

As important and valuable as this tool is for real estate investors, it is critical that you know your stuff. As with many things in real estate, a blunder or two can seriously backfire, damaging your deal and wreaking negative financial consequences. This is your guide to how self-directed retirement investing really works, when it makes sense to use or not, the other alternatives to tap into, what you can and can't do as a real estate investor, and where to find the experts who can help maximize your success.

NOTE:

Seek out professionals such as a CPA or tax attorney when complicated situations arise.

Chapter 2

History and Trends

"Understanding the history of self-directed IRAs is essential to mastering their potential. As regulations and market trends evolve, so do the strategies that allow investors to unlock the full power of retirement savings."

—On the Evolution of Financial Freedom

The retirement crisis is the largest and most urgent global crisis we face today.

The world's most respected economists and financial analysts warn of the pending retirement crisis. They are asking important questions that we as a nation should be asking: How did we land here? How have retirement plans evolved over the years? What risks and challenges do individuals face now? What emerging trends and strategies are arising that could save the global economy and your financial future?

With the "silver tsunami" crashing to the shore as more and more Baby Boomers hit their retirement years, the answers to the above questions become paramount. None of us wants to spend our golden years in a state-run facility. So take note.

To really get the value, importance, right perspective, and potential of SDIRA investing, it is critical to understand the history and emerging trends of retirement accounts. Here is a quick primer.

A Quick History of Retirement Accounts[1]

13 BCE:

Roman Emperor Augustus begins pensions for legionnaires with twenty years of service.

1st Century CE:

The New Testament pioneers the idea of tithing to help the poor and widows.

---

[1] John Iekel, "Retirement: An Historical Perspective," American Society of Pension Professionals & Actuaries, October 4, 2018, https://www.asppa-net.org/news/2018/10/retirement-historical-perspective/.

1717:

The Presbyterian Church begins a fund for retiring ministers.

1889:

If Plymouth colonists are wounded in combat, they receive a pension to support their families. However, the tax collection to raise these funds is often carried out by the "retired" veterans themselves.

1875:

The first private pension plan in America is created by the American Express Railroad.

1900:

Life expectancy is 49 years old, with retired workers generally being disabled.

1935:

Franklin D. Roosevelt signs the Social Security Act into law. The act provides a fixed income for the disabled and retired workers aged 65 and older. This is funded by a 1 percent tax on employees and their employers. By 2006, that tax had risen to 7.65 percent.

1974:

Tax-deductible IRAs are born.

1981:

401(k)s are established.

1997:

Roth IRAs are born.

2016:

The S&P Dow Jones Indices and MSCI move stock exchange–listed equity real estate investment trusts (REITs) and other listed real estate companies from the financials sector of their Global Industry Classification Standard (GICS®) to a new real estate sector.

2019:

The SECURE Act 1.0 pushes back the age at which retirement plan participants need to take required minimum distributions (RMDs) from 70½ to 72 and allows traditional IRA owners to keep making contributions indefinitely.

2022:

The SECURE Act 2.0 changes the age at which retirement account owners must begin taking RMDs. It is raised from 72 to 73 in 2023 and will increase to 75 in 2033. This gives savers more time to grow their accounts and defer taxes and may also help them preserve their savings longer and reduce their tax burden. The penalty for missed RMDs is reduced from 50 percent to 25 percent, and to 10 percent if the mistake is corrected quickly.

Looking back a couple of centuries, average people just never lived long enough to retire, nor were they simply dropping out to play golf and sip tea all day—a fantasy for which many people strive. They simply worked until they died.

The "golden years" was a term originally coined to refer to the peak working and earning years of 25 and 40. Now the term is used to describe a coveted period of relaxation, golfing, bingo, and travel retirees hope to achieve, but with plenty of income and no more workdays. If these are the golden years we all crave, why do we have to wait until we are elders to enjoy them? Isn't there a way to get there in our forties? The answer is yes, but it takes some planning ahead and smart investment decisions using an SDIRA.

Now we get to ask the really important question: How are Americans doing saving the finances they will need for a comfortable, timely retirement? With an estimated 10,000 baby boomers reaching the age of 65 every day for the next decade, this is a question in desperate need of an answer. This large sector of our aging population is composed of individuals with vastly underfunded pensions, and Social Security payouts aren't something most people can live on these days.

Retirees in greater numbers are forced out of their homes to live in RVs, vans, and cars. There is less and less stability. For many Americans, there is no such thing as a pension. Few companies offer such a safety net these days. If companies aren't taking care of their workers, who will? That's why taking retirement into our own hands is critical. That's what SDIRAs allow us to do.

As an investor, you have the opportunity to take control of your financial future by exploring self-directed retirement investing. By moving your typical brokerage retirement accounts into self-directed accounts, you can invest in "alternative assets," like real estate, in various forms. This approach not only offers the potential for higher returns but also acts as a safety net by diversifying your portfolio and reducing the risks associated with more conventional investments. By exploring these options, you can alleviate some of the fear and uncertainty that often comes with retirement planning.

The Current State of Retirement Savings

How Much Do Individuals Need to Retire?

Each individual's situation is unique, yet almost everyone underestimates how much money they will need to survive in their retirement years. In fact, the income truly needed can be a shock.

According to *Kiplinger's* retirement savings calculator, if you are 40 years old, plan to work until 70 and live until at least 90, you'll need a nest egg of almost $4.4 million.[2] That amount is just to maintain the same lifestyle you are living now. If you earn $100,000 per year now, *Kiplinger* says you'll need $243,000 per year in future dollars to afford the same lifestyle. The BiggerPockets *Money Show* podcast is a great resource to identify your personal financial goals and learn from the professionals how to effectively manage your money (www.BiggerPockets.com/BookMoneyPod). CNN Business's retirement calculator begins with a default nest egg of $100,000 for 35-year-olds, and a saving rate of 15 percent of income.

The data also shows a dramatic disparity between the expectations of spending in retirement and actual spending. On average, just two to four years after the average retirement age, the average retiree's account balance sinks by around 50 percent. These statistics are a big reality check, yet many people are still in the dark about them.

---

[2] Ellen Kennedy, "Retirement Savings Calculator: How Much Money Do I Need to Retire?" *Kiplinger Personal Finance*, August 22, 2024, https://www.kiplinger.com/retirement/retirement-planning/600895/retirement-savings-calculator.

How Much Do Individuals Really Save for Retirement?

In 2024, Vanguard reported the average 401(k) balance for 35- to 44-year-olds at $91,281.[3] For retirees (age 65 and up), the average is about $272,588. Yet that amount would barely yield $1,500 a month in income assuming retirement at 65 with a 15-year horizon. Vanguard reported the median 401(k) balance for those individuals with ten-plus years in the job force has reached $288,318. The time to start saving is now so you have more in your golden years.

Age Range	Average Balance	Median Balance
<25	$7,351	$2,856
25–34	$37,557	$14,933
35–44	$91,281	$35,537
45–54	$168,646	$60,763
55–64	$244,750	$87,571
65+	$272,583	$88,485

Table Source: Vanguard, How America Saves 2024

The Most Important Number in Retirement

What is more important to look at in your retirement portfolio: the size of your nest egg, your overall net worth, your returns, or your passive income?

MIT and Harvard professor and Nobel Prize winner Robert C. Merton says the answer is this: "The risk is retirement income uncertainty, not portfolio value." Based on Merton's conclusion, the most important number is "the amount of sustainable income an employee can expect to receive in retirement."[4]

Merton warns we are heading for a 401(k) crisis.[5] It is here already for many. But why?

The frightening shift is due in part to the dramatic shift from defined benefit plans to defined contribution plans, but also because 401(k)s and their reporting statements have individuals focusing on the

---

[3] Mallika Mitra, Paul Curcio, and David Tony, "How America Saves 2024," *Vanguard*, June 2024, https://corporate.vanguard.com/content/dam/corp/research/pdf/how_america_saves_report_2024.pdf.

[4] LSARET, "401(k)s Face 'Crisis,' Says Nobel Prize Winner Merton," *Wealth Strategies Journal*, June 25, 2014, https://wealthstrategiesjournal.com/2014/06/25/401ks-face-crisis-says-nobel-prize-winner-merton/.

[5] Penelope Wang, "This Nobel Economist Nails What's Really Wrong with Your 401(k)," Money.com, June 29, 2014, https://money.com/this-nobel-economist-nails-whats-really-wrong-with-your-401k/.

wrong goals. If everything is geared toward the size of the portfolio, it causes many to make the wrong choices for what is most critical—which is income. Merton isn't against a well-balanced portfolio that includes stocks. However, he is an advocate for deferred annuities and real estate, which he says can also be used as a pension as property owners tap into their property's equity during retirement.

Pensions and Investments magazine echoes this sentiment, saying, "Clearly, the risk and return variables that now drive investment decisions are not being measured in units that correspond to savers' retirement goals and their likelihood of meeting them. Thus, it cannot be said that savers' funds are being well managed."[6]

By taking control of their own investments, individuals can better diversify their holdings and optimize them as a strategy for growing wealth and maximizing passive income. This statement applies equally for those just starting out in a savings plan and those already on the verge of retirement.

CURVEBALLS AND CHALLENGES

There are a number of challenges facing individual investors today. The system appears to keep moving the goalposts further out, which just adds to the weight of the lead boots investors are being forced to slip into. If that's not enough, the bulk of the retirement and investment market not only appears to be weighted against making progress, but also to be leading many into a dense maze. Add what's going on in our current economic climate and the deck is stacked higher and higher against those who haven't taken time to think for themselves when it comes to their retirement and to use more out-of-the-box tools to get ahead earlier in life.

If individuals haven't resigned themselves to not receiving any government assistance in their retirement years, now is the time to get real.

The national workforce participation rate fell to just 62.7 percent in 2024.[7] That's the lowest since 1977.[8] Looking at the civilian labor

---

6 Frank Sortino and Hal Forsey, "Everyone Is Focusing on the Wrong Goal in Retirement Planning," *Pensions & Investments*, November 24, 2014, http://www.pionline.com/article/20141124/PRINT/311249997/everyone-is-focusing-on-the-wrong-goal-in-retirement-planning.

7 "Civilian Labor Force Participation Rate," U.S. Bureau of Labor Statistics, accessed September 16, 2024, https://www.bls.gov/charts/employment-situation/civilian-labor-force-participation-rate.htm.

8 Stephen Gandel, "America's Biggest Job Market Problem Is Uniquely American," *Fortune*, July 2, 2015, http://fortune.com/2015/07/02/us-labor-force-participation-drops/.

force participation rate data from the St. Louis Fed, if this downward trajectory continues along historical lines, it could once again fall below 60 percent. That's what happened from the late 1940s through mid-1960s.[9]

Civilian labor force participation rate, seasonally adjusted

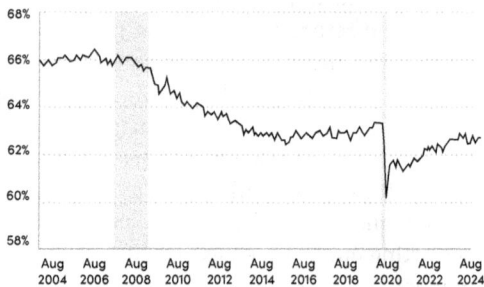

Image source: https://www.bls.gov/charts/employment-situation/civilian-labor-force-participation-rate.htm

For those thinking that they'll just work longer, the Economic History Association points out that the participation rate for men 65 and older plunged from almost 80 percent to just 17.5 percent between 1880 and 2000.[10] Fewer workers, workers participating in the workforce for fewer years, and the rising numbers of retirees are also resulting in rising costs. More money needs to be tapped from the active workforce in order to cover that gap. Realistically, individuals need to anticipate and prepare for less net earned income, higher expenses, and to work for fewer years.

As of 2023, participation in defined benefit pension plans had fallen to just 10 percent. Yet, what brings more risk is that there is very little guarantee of benefits. In the past, benefits would have been frozen during tough economic times. This is important to note, because at the time of this writing, a new tough economic period is heading our way. As a result, the Social Security Office of Retirement and Disability Policy has been running simulations on freezing all remaining

---

9   "Labor Force Participation Rate," FRED: Federal Reserve Bank of St. Louis, accessed September 16, 2024, https://fred.stlouisfed.org/series/CIVPART.

10   Joanna Short, "Economic History of Retirement in the United States," Economic History Association, accessed September 16, 2024, https://eh.net/encyclopedia/economic-history-of-retirement-in-the-united-states/.

private-sector and one-third of public-sector-defined benefit pension plans for five years.[11]

Financial leader Suze Orman warns, "In a traditional 401(k), what you see is not what you get." When discussing the biggest challenge, she notes, "You will have to pay taxes on that. At what rate? We don't know!" This may not play out as many expect due to the country's $35 trillion national debt.[12] Suze asks, "How [is the government] going to solve it? [Politicians] can say they're going to lower tax brackets, but we don't know that."[13]

The real curveball here is that evolving dynamics may be literally burning all the theories and calculations that individuals have relied on for their retirement planning. For example, Professor of Retirement Income at the American College of Financial Services Wade Pfau says, "Because interest rates are so low now, while stock markets are also very highly valued, we are in uncharted waters in terms of the conditions at the start of retirement and knowing whether the 4 percent rule can work in those cases."[14]

Add to this that living to the age of 100 and beyond is increasingly becoming a norm, while retiring at 65 is still the most likely age for Americans to take the plunge. Even if individuals plan to work until age 65, they will need the finances to provide a decent quality of life for 35 years of retirement. To get there, they will need to generate a lot more passive income from their earned income and investment returns. This is where self-directed retirement accounts are proving to be the much-needed ace up the sleeve for better-informed individual investors.

Emerging Economic Trends and Major Shifts

In addition to the age and workforce challenges, there are major economic and investment industry shifts that continue to evolve. You cannot ignore these trends, and burying your head in the sand

---

[11] Barbara A. Butrica et al., "The Disappearing Defined Benefit Pension and Its Potential Impact on the Retirement Incomes of Baby Boomers," *Social Security Bulletin* 69, no. 3 (2009), https://www.ssa.gov/policy/docs/ssb/v69n3/v69n3p1.html.

[12] "The National Debt Is Now More Than $35 Trillion. What Does That Mean?" Peter G. Peterson Foundation, July 29, 2024, https://www.pgpf.org/infographic/the-national-debt-is-now-more-than-35-trillion-what-does-that-mean.

[13] Nicole Spector, "Suze Orman: 'How Much Do I Need to Retire?' Is a Stupid Question! Here's How to Save," *Today*, September 25, 2015, https://www.today.com/money/suze-orman-how-much-do-i-need-retire-stupid-question-t45051.

[14] Stephen Gandel, "America's Biggest Job Market Problem is Uniquely American," *Fortune*, July 2 2015, https://fortune.com/2015/07/02/us-labor-force-participation-drops/.

will not help solve anything. Unless individuals take equally significant steps to counterbalance these trends and overprepare for their financial futures, they may find themselves woefully underprepared come retirement.

Perhaps most significantly, the nation's top financial minds and investment houses warn that we are entering a new era of low returns. Many in the financial realm, including PIMCO and Morgan Stanley, echo this sentiment. The *Financial Times* says low returns are the "new norm."[15] *Seeking Alpha* suggests we may be facing "a lost decade" for performance.[16] Former head of PIMCO Bill Gross recommends turning to real estate and even contemporary art to combat the declines and lack of returns from stocks and bonds. Even Warren Buffett has warned Berkshire Hathaway shareholders that lean times are on the horizon. Buffet has increased his personal and corporate investments in the real estate industry.

With a new recession and the potential for major corrections looming, individuals need to put some thought into preserving their portfolio and optimizing it for income in retirement. Even those in their thirties and forties really cannot afford another major dip in their portfolio values or a decade of zero returns.

In his book *Money*, Tony Robbins breaks through many myths and conventional wisdom associated with investing. Two of the most notable lessons from his interviews with the world's most successful financial experts and money managers are that we all need to understand how high fees impede results and how the ups and downs of market performance can impact real net returns. Robbins explains that few investors really understand how much they are paying in layers upon layers of fees.[17] If we are in an era where 3–5 percent growth is optimistic in the stock market and investors are paying at least that much in fees, that means zero net gains. Wow! What a revelation.

In fact, once you understand that last statement, you know that it means losing money due to inflation. Benjamin Graham's principle of dollar-cost averaging is often thrown around as a reason why investors shouldn't pull out during market dips and major sell-offs. Yet, even

---

[15] Hugo Greenhalgh, "Low Returns Will Be New Norm for Investors, Say Wealth Managers," *Financial Times*, February 2, 2016, http://www.ft.com/cms/s/0/12df0d5c-c9a3-11e5-a8ef-ea66e967dd44.html#axzz3zblTXln2.

[16] Roger Nusbaum, "Is A Lost Decade for Performance Coming?" *Seeking Alpha*, April 2, 2015, http://seekingalpha.com/article/3048776-is-a-lost-decade-for-performance-coming.

[17] Tony Robbins, *Money: Master the Game* (Simon & Schuster, 2014).

if you cannot perfect timing of trades, it does not require a financial genius to figure out that a 50 percent drop in your stock portfolio value is going to require years of gains to recuperate before getting back to par. If the market drops 50 percent this year, and goes up 10 percent per year for the next five years, you are still in the red. In fact, you are still down by almost 20 percent! Don't forget to subtract fees and taxes on those gains too.

In recent years, large hedge funds and pension funds have significantly increased their allocations to real estate. This is driven by the asset's perceived stability amid volatile market conditions, making it a popular choice for those seeking a hedge against risk. Major pension funds such as the California Public Employees' Retirement System (CalPERS) and prominent firms, like Blackstone, continue to expand their real estate portfolios.[18] In 2024, U.S. pension funds have notably raised their real estate investments, motivated by the need to counterbalance the risks present in other sectors.[19]

Canadian pension funds also remain key players in global real estate markets, with institutions like the Ontario Teachers' Pension Plan and the Canada Pension Plan Investment Board ranking among the largest property investors globally. Their consistent focus on prime real estate markets, including high-profile acquisitions in cities like Manhattan, demonstrates their confidence in the long-term value of real estate.[20]

At the same time, the shift toward remote work has transformed how individuals plan for retirement. With more people working remotely, retirees are now considering relocating to areas with lower living costs, leveraging the flexibility to stretch their retirement savings while maintaining a desirable quality of life. In 2024, a substantial portion of remote workers are high-earning, white-collar professionals, which provides opportunities for independent contractors and small business owners to contribute more to self-directed retirement accounts, such as solo 401(k)s and IRAs.

---

[18] Robert Campbell and Lola Panagos, "US Pension Funds Up Real Estate Exposure to Offset Rising Risks," *S&P Global*, August 18, 2024, https://www.spglobal.com/marketintelligence/en/news-insights/latest-news-headlines/us-pension-funds-up-real-estate-exposure-to-offset-rising-risks-71610560.

[19] "5 Hedge Funds Investing in Real Estate in 2024," *The Adviser Magazine*, February 2024, https://theadvisermagazine.com/market-research/investing/5-hedge-funds-investing-in-real-estate-in-2024/.

[20] Campbell and Panagos, "US Pension Funds."

Moreover, as stock market volatility continues to affect traditional portfolios, more investors are turning to self-directed retirement accounts. These vehicles, which allow for greater flexibility in choosing asset classes like real estate, are gaining visibility, especially as economic uncertainty drives demand for diversified investment strategies. This shift highlights the growing need for guidance and education on self-directed investing.

Taking Control with Self-Directed Retirement Accounts

Taking the reins of your financial future, investment performance, lifestyle in retirement, and legacy can be far easier than you may realize.

Those with existing retirement accounts can roll them over into self-directed variations. Individuals just starting out can choose from several types of self-directed individual retirement accounts, which can be set up at any time. This includes salaried workers, small business owners, independent entrepreneurs, and spouses.

The option to use SDIRAs has gained significant attention in the media, with coverage from outlets like *Bankrate*, *Fox Business*, and *Forbes*. This growing interest reflects the powerful potential of SDIRAs to enhance your investment strategy. By leveraging the tax advantages offered by these accounts, investors can potentially boost their net returns by 20 percent or more annually, as profits are either tax deferred or tax free (depending on whether you're using a traditional or Roth IRA). This strategy can significantly increase your long-term wealth, making SDIRAs an appealing option for those looking to maximize their retirement savings.

With the assistance of a reputable and seasoned IRA custodian, individuals can select from a much broader range of investment options.

Basically, an IRA custodian is a financial institution that holds your account's investments for safekeeping and provides oversight and tax reporting. (Note that it is up to the account holder to make sure they adhere to all IRS and government regulations at all times.)

Individuals can leverage professional advisors and asset managers/management companies, or they can invest directly to slash fees and retain more of their gains. They can do all of this while insulating themselves from the taxman—legally. Read more about tax benefits of SDIRAs in Chapter 5.

Investing in Real Estate

Investment in real estate has continued its strong growth, driven by its ability to offer security, diversification, and stable returns. In 2023, U.S. commercial real estate investment volume reached $710 billion, an increase from $646 billion in 2022, according to the National Association of Realtors.[21] Real estate provides advantages like consistent cash flow from rental income and potential property appreciation. Unlike stocks or bonds, real estate allows for direct control over assets, making it an attractive option for investors seeking less volatility and tangible returns.

Top financial leaders continue to invest heavily in real estate. Hedge fund managers like Bill Ackman and Blackstone's Stephen Schwarzman have made headline-grabbing purchases, illustrating the continued appeal of prime real estate among high-net-worth individuals.[22] Mark Zuckerberg, for example, has built an extensive real estate portfolio, further emphasizing how real estate remains a key wealth-building strategy.[23]

With new technology improving the ease, efficiency, and profitability of investing in real estate, the attraction to this asset class is likely to keep growing.

How can individuals pull it all together and combine the benefits of investing in real estate and the tax shelter of self-directed retirement accounts?

Keep reading. That's what I'll go into next.

---

[21] "Understand Market Behavior: Research and Statistics," NAR: National Association of Realtors, accessed September 23, 2024, https://www.nar.realtor/research-and-statistics.

[22] Robert Campbell and Lola Panagos, "US pension funds up real estate exposure to offset rising risks," S&P Global, August 18, 2022, https://www.spglobal.com/marketintelligence/en/news-insights/latestnews-headlines/us-pension-funds-up-real-estateexposure-to-offset-rising-risks-71610560.

[23] Jordan Hart, "Mark Zuckerberg Owns over 1,200 Acres of Land. Here's a Look at His Properties Across the US, from a Hawaiian Doomsday Bunker to Lake Tahoe Estates," Business Insider, April 7, 2024, https://www.businessinsider.com/inside-mark-zuckerbergs-extensive-real-estate-portfolio-2024-4.

Chapter 3

SDIRA Foundations—Using IRA Accounts

> "The more due diligence, the more education, the more research you've done, usually the better your result."

SDIRAs are a powerful tool for individual investors, real estate promoters, and industry vendors. But how do they work? How do the different types of accounts that are available stack up? What can and cannot be done with them?

> I will mention throughout this book how important it is in many situations to consult with competent tax and financial professionals. There is a free and straightforward way to do so through the BiggerPockets financial services finder, at **www.BiggerPockets.com/BookCPA.**

Types of Self-Directed Retirement Accounts

SDIRAs go by different names for promotional purposes. Some of them are just names and really refer to the generic self-directed IRA. The term "self-directed IRA" or SDIRA is also often used to describe this suite of tools in general, though some of the specifics may vary.

Types of self-directed accounts available today:

- Individual or solo 401(k)
- Traditional IRA
- Roth IRA
- Spousal IRA
- SEP IRA
- SIMPLE IRA
- Employer plans (covered in Chapter 4)
- Health savings plan (HSA) (covered in Chapter 4)
- Education savings account (Coverdell) (covered in Chapter 4)
- Self-directed account for minors (covered in Chapter 4)

Individual 401(k)

Also known as a solo 401(k) for an individual, the individual 401(k) is the newest and most exciting retirement plan to benefit the self-employed, all thanks to the tax law created by the Economic Growth and Tax Relief Reconciliation Act of 2001 (EGTRRA). This tax law became effective on January 1, 2002, and provides significant advantages to small businesses whose only employee is the owner or the owner and their spouse. These self-employed business owners can establish an individual 401(k) plan and take advantage of this powerful retirement savings tool. It is the entrepreneurs' pension plan.

What makes the individual 401(k) unique is that, compared to other self-employed retirement plans greater contributions may be made at identical income levels, thereby maximizing retirement contributions and valuable tax deductions.

Solo 401(k) contribution limits change each year. For 2025, the employee (participant) portion is $23,500 for those under 50 and $31,000 for those over 50. The total contribution to a solo 401(k) is the lesser of 25 percent of your income up to a cap of $70,000. The annual solo 401(k) contribution consists of two parts: a salary-deferral contribution and a profit-sharing contribution. The total allowable contribution adds these two parts together to get to the maximum solo 401(k) contribution limit.

Solo 401(k) contributions are flexible. Both salary-deferral and profit-sharing contributions are discretionary and can be changed at any time based on business profitability.

The contribution limits can be doubled for husband-and-wife businesses. Additionally, businesses with a spouse on the payroll can also contribute to the solo 401(k). In that case, there would be one solo 401(k) for the business, with two participants.

Self-employed business owners with no W-2 employees may be well suited for an individual 401(k) if their objective is to maximize their retirement contributions or if they would like to borrow from their retirement plan using their 401(k) balance as collateral via a tax-free individual 401(k) loan. You will learn more about the solo 401(k) in Chapter 15.

Traditional IRA

The traditional individual retirement account (IRA) is one of the most common and widely used retirement accounts in the United States. This popularity is largely due to the ease with which individuals can roll over their employer-sponsored retirement accounts, such as 401(k)s, into a traditional IRA after leaving a job or retiring. The key advantage of a traditional IRA is the potential for a tax deduction on contributions for those who qualify, which makes it an attractive option for individuals seeking to reduce their taxable income.

WHAT IS A TRADITIONAL IRA?

A traditional IRA is a type of retirement savings account that allows individuals to make contributions using pretax dollars. The funds in a traditional IRA grow tax deferred, meaning that the investments within the account can appreciate without being subject to taxes until withdrawals are made. This tax-deferred growth can significantly enhance the compounding effect, allowing your investments to grow faster over time.

When you eventually withdraw money from a traditional IRA, typically after the age of 59½, the withdrawals are taxed as ordinary income based on your current tax rate at that time. It's important to note that any withdrawals made before reaching the age of 59½ are generally subject to an early withdrawal penalty of 10 percent in addition to being taxed as ordinary income.

KEY FEATURES AND RULES OF TRADITIONAL IRAS

To fully understand the benefits and requirements of a traditional IRA, it's essential to familiarize yourself with the rules outlined in IRS Publication 590-A and Publication 590-B. These publications cover a range of topics related to IRAs, including:

- **Setting up an IRA:** Establishing a traditional IRA is a straightforward process. You can open an account with a variety of financial institutions, such as self-directed retirement companies, banks, credit unions, mutual fund companies, or brokerage firms.
- **Contributing to an IRA:** For 2024/25, the contribution limit for a traditional IRA is $7,000 for individuals under the age of 50. If you are 50 or older, you can make an additional catch-up contribution of $1,000, bringing the total contribution limit to $8,000. It's important to note that these limits are adjusted annually for inflation, so they may change in subsequent years.

Starting in 2025, individuals aged 60 to 63 will have the opportunity to make enhanced "catch-up" contributions to their retirement accounts. They can contribute either $10,000 or 150 percent of the standard catch-up contribution limit for those aged 50 and older, whichever is higher. This amount will be adjusted annually for inflation, enabling these individuals to save substantially more during this critical pre-retirement period.

- **Transferring money or property to and from an IRA:** You can transfer or roll over funds from other retirement accounts, such as a 401(k) or another IRA, into a traditional IRA without incurring taxes or penalties, as long as you follow IRS rules. This process is commonly referred to as a "rollover."
- **Handling an inherited IRA:** If you inherit a traditional IRA, there are specific rules and options for handling the account, depending on whether you are a spouse or a non-spouse beneficiary. It's important to understand these rules to avoid unintended taxes or penalties.
- **Receiving distributions from an IRA:** Once you reach the age of 59½, you can begin taking distributions from your traditional IRA without incurring the early withdrawal penalty. However, you will still need to pay ordinary income tax on the amounts withdrawn. Required minimum distributions (RMDs) begin at age 73, meaning you must start withdrawing a minimum amount each year, whether you need the money or not.
- **Taking a credit for contributions to an IRA:** Some individuals may be eligible for a tax credit, known as the Saver's Credit, for making contributions to a traditional IRA. This credit can reduce your overall tax liability, providing an additional incentive to save for retirement.
- **Comparison of traditional and Roth IRAs:** While both traditional and Roth IRAs offer valuable retirement savings options, there are key differences in how they are taxed. Contributions to a traditional IRA are typically made with pretax dollars, and withdrawals in retirement are taxed as ordinary income.

Roth IRA

THE ROTH INDIVIDUAL RETIREMENT ACCOUNT (IRA)

The Roth individual retirement account (IRA) is a unique retirement savings vehicle that offers different tax advantages compared to other types of IRAs. Unlike traditional IRAs and other retirement plans, which provide tax-deferred growth, a Roth IRA allows for tax-free growth. This means that because contributions to a Roth IRA are made with after-tax dollars, the funds within the account grow tax-free, and qualified withdrawals are not taxed.

This feature makes the Roth IRA particularly attractive to individuals who expect to be in a higher tax bracket in the future or who value the flexibility of tax-free withdrawals. The Roth IRA, governed by rules outlined in IRS Publication 590, can be a powerful tool for building wealth and planning for retirement, especially for those who anticipate significant growth in their investments.

WHAT IS A ROTH IRA?

A Roth IRA is a type of retirement account that allows individuals to contribute after-tax dollars, with the promise of tax-free withdrawals in retirement. Contributions to a Roth IRA do not provide an immediate tax deduction, as they are made with income that has already been taxed. However, the significant benefit of a Roth IRA is that the investments within the account grow tax free, and qualified distributions are also tax free.

This is in contrast to a traditional IRA, where contributions may be tax deductible, but withdrawals are taxed as ordinary income. Roth IRAs also offer more flexibility regarding withdrawals, as contributions (but not earnings) can be withdrawn at any time without penalty, providing liquidity and access to funds if needed. There is a caveat that you must have owned the account for at least five years for this to apply.

KEY FEATURES OF A ROTH IRA

Tax-Free Growth and Withdrawals

The defining characteristic of a Roth IRA is that earnings within the account grow tax free, and qualified withdrawals are not subject to taxes. A qualified distribution is one that is made after the account has been open for at least five years and the account holder is at least 59½ years old. Distributions may also be qualified if the account holder becomes disabled, passes away, or uses up to $10,000 for a first-time home purchase.

Because of this tax treatment, Roth IRAs are particularly beneficial for individuals who expect their investments to appreciate significantly or who believe they will be in a higher tax bracket in retirement. By paying taxes up front at their current rate, they can avoid paying potentially higher taxes on their investment gains in the future.

No Required Minimum Distributions (RMDs)

Unlike traditional IRAs, Roth IRAs do not have required minimum distributions (RMDs). This means that individuals can leave their funds in the Roth IRA for as long as they wish, allowing for continued tax-free growth. This feature makes Roth IRAs a valuable estate-planning tool, as the funds can be passed on to heirs with minimal tax implications.

Flexible Contribution and Income Limits

For 2024/25, individuals can contribute up to $7,000 to a Roth IRA, with an additional catch-up contribution of $1,000 allowed for those aged 50 and older, bringing the total to $8,000. However, contributions to a Roth IRA are subject to income limits. For single filers, the ability to contribute to a Roth IRA begins to phase out at a modified adjusted gross income (MAGI) of $150,000 and is completely phased out at $165,000. For married couples filing jointly, the phaseout range is between $236,000 and $246,000. These limitations change annually, so be sure to discuss them with your competent tax professional.

Roth Contributions Can Be Taken Out at Any Time Without Penalty

One of the key benefits of a Roth IRA is the flexibility it offers with contributions. Unlike other retirement accounts, contributions made to a Roth IRA can be withdrawn at any time, for any reason, without penalty or taxes. This is because contributions are made with after-tax dollars, meaning the taxes have already been paid. However, it's important to note that this flexibility applies only to contributions, not to earnings on those contributions, which may be subject to taxes and penalties if withdrawn before age 59½ and before the account has been open for at least five years. This feature makes Roth IRAs a useful tool for those who want to save for retirement while maintaining access to their funds if needed.

WHO SHOULD CHOOSE A ROTH IRA?

A Roth IRA can be an excellent choice for various individuals, depending on their financial situation, income level, and future tax expectations.

Lower-Income Individuals

For individuals in lower tax brackets, particularly those with little or no tax liability, a Roth IRA can be a smart choice. Since these individuals are already in a low tax bracket, the immediate tax deduction offered by a traditional IRA provides minimal benefit. By choosing a Roth IRA instead, they can benefit from tax-free growth and withdrawals in the future when their tax rate may be higher.

Young Entrepreneurs and Investors in Start-Ups

According to experts like Sandeep and Sanjeev Sardana of BluePointe Capital Management, a Roth IRA is an excellent vehicle for young entrepreneurs or investors looking to invest in start-ups or private small business stock.[24] Because contributions to a Roth IRA are made with after-tax dollars and the investments grow tax free, any large gains realized from investments in start-ups can be withdrawn tax free, provided they meet the qualified distribution criteria.

This strategy can be particularly advantageous for young investors who may not have significant income or tax liability in their early years but who anticipate substantial growth in their investments. By utilizing a Roth IRA, they can shelter these gains from taxes, maximizing their investment returns far ahead of retirement age.

High-Income Earners with Strategic Tax Planning

On the other hand, high-income earners in higher tax brackets may prefer a traditional IRA to take advantage of the immediate tax deduction, reducing their taxable income in the year of contribution. This strategy can be particularly effective for those who anticipate being in a lower tax bracket during retirement, allowing them to minimize their overall tax liability.

By deferring taxes until retirement, high-income earners can plan to withdraw funds when their income is lower, and they are potentially subject to lower tax rates. This approach requires careful planning

---

[24] Sanjeev and Sandeep Sardana, "A Compelling Reason To Use Your Roth IRA To Fund Your Startup," *Forbes*, February 22, 2016, https://www.forbes.com/sites/sanjeevsardana/2016/02/22/compelling-reason-to-use-your-roth-ira-to-fund-your-startup/.

and consideration of future income sources, potential RMDs, and overall tax strategy.

INVESTING IN START-UPS WITH A ROTH IRA

One of the unique advantages of a Roth IRA is its potential use as a vehicle for investing in start-ups or private small business stock. For young entrepreneurs and investors with little current income or tax liability, a Roth IRA can be an excellent way to shelter potential gains from taxes.

For example, an individual could use Roth IRA funds to invest in a private small business, such as a start-up. If the business grows significantly and the investment appreciates, the gains can be withdrawn tax free, provided the account meets the qualified distribution requirements. This strategy allows investors to take advantage of the tax-free growth potential of a Roth IRA while also supporting entrepreneurial ventures.

However, it's essential to consider the implications of the PATH Act of 2015 (still in force in 2024). This act made 100 percent of gains on qualified small business stock tax free up to a $10 million threshold. This means that, in some cases, there may be overlapping benefits between the tax treatment of gains from qualified small business stock and the tax-free growth of a Roth IRA. Investors should consult with a tax professional to understand the full implications of these rules and how best to leverage them in their financial planning.

CONSIDERATIONS AND LIMITATIONS

Income Limits and Contribution Phases

Roth IRAs are subject to income limits, which can restrict who is eligible to contribute directly to a Roth IRA. High-income earners who exceed the phaseout thresholds may not be able to contribute directly to a Roth IRA. However, there are strategies, such as the "backdoor" Roth IRA conversion that can allow these individuals to take advantage of the benefits of a Roth IRA by converting a traditional IRA into a Roth IRA, though this may trigger taxes on the converted amount.

Immediate Tax Impact

Unlike a traditional IRA, contributions to a Roth IRA do not provide an immediate tax deduction. For individuals in higher tax brackets, this could mean a higher tax bill in the year of contribution. This trade-off must be considered when deciding between a Roth IRA and a traditional IRA, particularly for those who need to reduce their taxable income in the short term.

Five-Year Clock

The Roth IRA five-year clock is a key rule investors must understand when contributing to or withdrawing from their Roth IRA accounts. This rule essentially sets a timeline that determines whether withdrawals from a Roth IRA are considered "qualified" and therefore tax and penalty free. The five-year clock starts ticking on January 1 of the year for which your first Roth IRA contribution is made. For example, if you make a Roth contribution for the year 2025, your five-year period begins on January 1, 2025, regardless of when during the year you made the contribution. The same five-year rule applies to Roth IRA conversions.

For contributions, the rule ensures that withdrawals of earnings are tax free after five years, provided you meet other criteria, such as being 59½ or older. For conversions, each conversion starts its own five-year clock, and withdrawals of converted amounts could be subject to penalties if taken out before five years, though they are not subject to income tax (since taxes were paid upon conversion). Understanding how the five-year clock applies to your contributions, conversions, and withdrawals can help you optimize the tax benefits of your Roth IRA and avoid potential penalties.

Qualified Distributions

While Roth IRAs offer tax-free withdrawals, it's important to understand the rules surrounding qualified distributions. For a distribution to be qualified, the account must have been open for at least five years, and the distribution must occur after the account holder reaches 59½ years of age or meets other qualifying conditions. Early withdrawals of earnings that do not meet these criteria may be subject to taxes and penalties.

The Backdoor Roth IRA

In navigating the world of retirement savings, you may have heard of a "backdoor" Roth IRA. While it sounds like a specific type of retirement account, it's actually a strategy that allows high-income earners who surpass the income limits for Roth IRA contributions to fund a Roth IRA indirectly. This is accomplished by converting a traditional IRA into a Roth IRA.

Roth conversions allow funds from SIMPLE or SEP IRAs to be converted into a Roth IRA, enabling tax-free growth and withdrawals in retirement. While taxes are due on the converted amount, this strategy can be beneficial for those seeking to diversify their retirement savings with tax-advantaged options.

It's important to note that this strategy is not a tax loophole but rather a legal approach made possible by the Tax Increase Prevention and Reconciliation Act (TIPRA). When you convert a traditional IRA to a Roth IRA, you're required to pay taxes on any funds that haven't yet been taxed. This includes both the initial contributions and any earnings or appreciation on those contributions. If your traditional IRA was funded with tax-deductible contributions, the entire amount transferred will be subject to taxes. However, the advantage of a Roth IRA is that once taxes are paid on the conversion, future withdrawals can be tax free, as long as you follow the applicable rules.

Main Points:

- The backdoor Roth IRA enables high-income earners to convert a traditional IRA into a Roth IRA.
- You can contribute to a traditional IRA, convert it to a Roth IRA, and bypass the Roth IRA income limits.
- This strategy is perfectly legal but does have immediate tax implications from the conversion. It also offers long-term tax benefits, like tax-free withdrawals.
- The backdoor Roth IRA is especially useful for individuals who expect to leave leftover IRA funds to heirs, as Roth IRAs provide tax-free inheritance benefits.

HOW THE BACKDOOR ROTH IRA WORKS

Roth IRAs allow you to contribute after-tax dollars, meaning the money you put in has already been taxed, and future withdrawals are tax free. This is different from traditional IRAs, where contributions may be tax deductible, and taxes are only paid when you withdraw the funds. However, for high-income earners, direct contributions to Roth IRAs phase out above certain income levels.

Traditional IRAs, on the other hand, have no income limits. Since 2010, the IRS has permitted anyone—regardless of income—to convert a traditional IRA into a Roth IRA. This provision opens the door to the backdoor Roth IRA strategy, making it an option for those unable to contribute directly to a Roth IRA due to income restrictions.

STEPS TO CREATE A BACKDOOR ROTH IRA

1. Contribute to a traditional IRA or an SEP IRA: You can contribute up to the annual limit in a traditional IRA.
2. Convert to a Roth IRA: Convert as much as you like, even beyond the annual contribution limit. This is one of the main appeals of this strategy.
3. Roll over a 401(k): If your company's 401(k) plan allows it, you can roll over your 401(k) funds into a Roth IRA as well.
4. Pay taxes on any untaxed funds.

It's advisable to consult with your IRA custodian or financial advisor to ensure the conversion process is handled smoothly and in compliance with tax regulations.

TAX IMPLICATIONS OF A BACKDOOR ROTH IRA

The act of converting a traditional IRA into a Roth IRA will trigger taxes on any untaxed contributions or earnings. For example, if you contributed $7,000 to a traditional IRA and deducted it from your taxes, converting that $7,000 to a Roth IRA will create a tax obligation. The same applies to any earnings the account has accumulated between the time of the contribution and conversion.

However, if your traditional IRA was funded with after-tax contributions, you won't be taxed again on those amounts when they are converted. Keep in mind that most traditional IRAs are funded with pretax contributions, which means a significant portion of your conversion could be taxable. Also, converting a substantial amount at once could potentially push you into a higher tax bracket.

The IRS uses a pro rata rule to ensure that any after-tax contributions are not taxed again during the conversion process. This calculation is crucial in determining which part of the conversion is subject to taxes.

One additional detail to remember: Any funds converted to a Roth IRA must remain in the account for at least five years before they can be withdrawn penalty free if you are under the age of 59½. This five-year rule applies to converted funds, which are treated differently from regular Roth IRA contributions, which can generally be withdrawn at any time without taxes or penalties.

BENEFITS OF A BACKDOOR ROTH IRA

Why go through the hassle of a backdoor Roth IRA? The main benefit lies in the long-term advantages. For one, Roth IRAs have no required minimum distributions (RMDs), allowing you to leave the funds to grow tax free for as long as you live. This feature is particularly beneficial for those who don't plan on using all their retirement funds and may want to leave an inheritance to heirs.

Additionally, Roth IRAs offer tax-free withdrawals. After you pay taxes at the time of conversion, all future earnings and withdrawals are tax free. This can lead to substantial tax savings over the years, especially if you expect tax rates to rise or if you anticipate a higher income in retirement.

IS A BACKDOOR ROTH IRA STILL ALLOWED?

Yes, the backdoor Roth IRA strategy remains legal as of now. There are no restrictions imposed by the IRS on this practice, making it a valuable tool for high-income earners seeking tax-advantaged retirement savings.

IS A BACKDOOR ROTH IRA A GOOD IDEA?

For high earners, a backdoor Roth IRA can be an excellent strategy to take advantage of the long-term tax benefits of a Roth account. If you're unable to contribute directly to a Roth IRA due to income limitations, this approach allows you to bypass those restrictions while enjoying tax-free growth and withdrawals in retirement. This strategy is particularly advantageous in a year when you also have a loss to report on your taxes, as a Roth conversion during such a year can minimize the tax impact. Additionally, a backdoor Roth IRA provides flexibility in managing your retirement savings, which can be especially valuable if you're concerned about rising future tax rates.

DO YOU PAY TAXES TWICE ON A BACKDOOR ROTH IRA?

No. When you convert pretax contributions from a traditional IRA to a Roth IRA, you pay taxes on the converted amount. Once that tax is paid, all future withdrawals from the Roth IRA will be tax free.

Before diving into a backdoor Roth IRA, it's crucial to evaluate the tax consequences. Converting a significant balance from a traditional IRA to a Roth IRA could result in a hefty tax bill up front. However, the long-term advantages, such as tax-free withdrawals, no required minimum distributions, and tax-free inheritance benefits, often outweigh the initial tax hit. For high-income earners, particularly those planning to leave an inheritance or who anticipate a higher tax environment in the future, a backdoor Roth IRA can be an excellent strategy for securing tax-free retirement savings.

The Roth IRA, with its combination of tax-free growth, flexible withdrawal options, and lack of required minimum distributions provides a powerful tool for long-term retirement planning and wealth building.

CONVERTING A 529 PLAN TO ROTH

Starting in 2024, a significant change in the tax code allows savers to convert unused 529 plan funds into retirement savings by rolling them into a Roth IRA, offering a new level of flexibility in financial planning. This new rule permits up to $35,000 in lifetime rollovers from a 529 plan to a Roth IRA, giving those who may not fully use their 529 funds—due to scholarships, lower-than-expected education costs, or other reasons—a way to repurpose that money for retirement. This change eliminates the worry of potential tax penalties or restrictions on excess 529 funds, allowing parents and beneficiaries to secure their financial future in a different way.

However, there are important conditions for this rollover. First, the 529 plan must be at least fifteen years old to qualify, and only funds that have been in the plan for more than five years can be rolled over. The rollover counts toward the annual Roth IRA contribution limit, which for 2024 is set at $7,000 (with an additional $1,000 catch-up contribution allowed for those aged 50 and older). The beneficiary of the 529 plan must also be the one who owns the Roth IRA, and the total lifetime rollover cap remains $35,000. By understanding these nuances, investors can potentially turn unused education savings into a valuable tool for retirement, adding an extra layer of tax-advantaged growth to their portfolio.

Consulting with a financial advisor can help ensure you navigate the rules effectively and make the most of this new opportunity.

Spousal IRA

A spousal IRA is another powerful retirement savings tool specifically designed for married couples where one spouse is not earning income. The concept behind a spousal IRA is to allow a nonworking or lower-earning spouse to contribute to an individual retirement account (IRA), thereby enabling both spouses to maximize their retirement savings. This account can be set up as a traditional IRA, Roth IRA, or SDIRA, depending on the couple's financial goals and tax considerations.

WHAT IS A SPOUSAL IRA?

Despite its name, a spousal IRA is not a distinct type of IRA but rather a special provision that allows a nonworking spouse to contribute to an IRA based on the working spouse's income. In essence, it enables a married couple to double their IRA contributions, enhancing their retirement savings potential.

The spousal IRA can be established as a:

- Traditional IRA: Contributions may be tax deductible, and the investments grow tax deferred until withdrawals are made.
- Roth IRA: Contributions are made with after-tax dollars, and qualified withdrawals in retirement are tax free.
- SDIRA: This version allows for a broader range of investment options, including real estate, private equity, and more, giving the account holder greater control over their investment strategy.

HOW DOES A SPOUSAL IRA WORK?

To contribute to a spousal IRA, the following conditions must be met:

- Marital status: The couple must be legally married and file a joint tax return.
- Income requirements: The working spouse must have sufficient earned income to cover both their contribution and the contribution to the spousal IRA. Earned income includes wages, salaries, tips, commissions, and self-employment income.
- Age and contribution limits: Contribution limits for spousal IRAs are the same as for regular IRAs. For 2024, the maximum contribution is $7,000 per person if under

50 years of age and $8,000 if 50 or older. This means that, together, a couple can contribute up to $14,000 or $16,000 if both are 50 or older.

BENEFITS OF A SPOUSAL IRA

- Maximizing retirement savings: A spousal IRA allows a couple to contribute to two separate IRA accounts, effectively doubling the amount they can save for retirement each year. This is especially beneficial for households where one spouse is not working or earns significantly less.
- Tax benefits: Depending on the type of IRA chosen, contributions to a spousal IRA can provide immediate tax benefits. For a traditional IRA, contributions may be tax-deductible, reducing the couple's taxable income for the year. For a Roth IRA, while contributions are not tax deductible, the potential for tax-free withdrawals in retirement can be advantageous, particularly if the couple expects to be in a higher tax bracket later in life.
- Flexibility in investment choices: With the option to establish an SDIRA, couples have the flexibility to invest in a wide range of assets, including real estate, private companies, precious metals, and more. This diversification can be a key factor in building a robust retirement portfolio.

CONTRIBUTION AND DEDUCTION LIMITS

The contribution and deduction rules for a spousal IRA vary depending on whether it is a traditional or Roth IRA.

Traditional IRA: Contributions to a spousal IRA may be fully or partially deductible, depending on the working spouse's income and whether they are covered by a retirement plan at work. For 2025, the income limits for a full deduction are:

- If neither spouse is covered by a retirement plan at work, the contribution is fully deductible, regardless of income.
- If the working spouse is covered by a retirement plan, the deduction is phased out for couples with a modified adjusted gross income (MAGI) between $123,000 and $143,000.

- If the working spouse is not covered by a retirement plan but the nonworking spouse is, the deduction is phased out for MAGI between $230,000 and $240,000.

Roth IRA: Contributions to a Roth IRA are not tax deductible, but eligibility to contribute is based on income limits.

- For 2025, married couples filing jointly can contribute the maximum amount to a Roth IRA if their MAGI is below $230,000. The contribution limit phases out between $230,000 and $240,000.

ESTABLISHING A SPOUSAL IRA

Setting up a spousal IRA involves the same steps as establishing any IRA.

1. Choose the type of IRA: Decide whether to open a traditional, Roth, or SDIRA based on your financial goals, tax considerations, and investment strategy.
2. Select a financial institution: Choose a bank, credit union, brokerage firm, or other financial institution to open your IRA. For SDIRAs, you will need a custodian who specializes in handling these accounts.
3. Complete the application: Provide the necessary personal and financial information to open the account.
4. Make contributions: Begin contributing to the spousal IRA based on the eligible limits and guidelines.
5. Disclose your spousal IRA to your tax professional so you receive the appropriate tax credit/savings.

IMPORTANT CONSIDERATIONS

- Early withdrawals: Withdrawals from a spousal IRA before the age of 59½ may be subject to a 10 percent early withdrawal penalty, in addition to income taxes, if it is a traditional IRA. Exceptions may apply in certain circumstances, such as disability or first-time home purchase.
- Required minimum distributions (RMDs): Traditional IRAs require account holders to begin taking RMDs starting at age 73. Roth IRAs do not have RMDs during the

account holder's lifetime, which can make them a strategic choice for those seeking to minimize taxes and maximize growth potential.

- Income limitations: The ability to deduct contributions or contribute to a Roth IRA may be limited based on the couple's income. It's important to consult with a tax advisor or financial planner to understand the specific implications for your situation.

The SEP IRA

The Simplified Employee Pension individual retirement account (SEP IRA) is a powerful retirement savings tool designed primarily for business owners, self-employed individuals, and their employees. SEP IRAs allow for much higher contribution limits compared to traditional IRAs, making them an attractive option for those looking to maximize their retirement savings while enjoying significant tax advantages. This type of IRA is particularly beneficial for small business owners and real estate professionals who want to increase their contributions substantially and potentially reduce their taxable income.

WHAT IS A SEP IRA?

A SEP IRA is a retirement plan that allows business owners and self-employed individuals to contribute to their own retirement savings as well as those of their employees. Contributions to a SEP IRA are made by the employer and are typically tax deductible, which can provide a significant tax break. One of the key features of a SEP IRA is its high contribution limit, which can be up to 25 percent of the employee's compensation or a maximum amount set by the IRS each year, whichever is less.

For 2024, the maximum contribution limit for a SEP IRA is the lesser of 25 percent of compensation or $69,000—significantly higher than the contribution limits for traditional and Roth IRAs. This allows business owners and self-employed individuals to potentially contribute up to ten times more than they could with a traditional IRA, dramatically accelerating their retirement savings.

SEP ROTH IRA CONTRIBUTIONS

Starting after December 31, 2022, SEP IRAs and SIMPLE IRAs can be designated as Roth IRAs. Roth contributions are made with after-tax dollars, meaning the money is taxed before it goes into the retirement account. The key benefit of Roth accounts is that, provided certain conditions are met, withdrawals during retirement are tax free, including both contributions and earnings. This can be especially advantageous for those who anticipate being in a higher tax bracket during retirement.

KEY FEATURES OF A SEP IRA

High Contribution Limits

The most notable feature of a SEP IRA is its high contribution limits. This provides a substantial opportunity for business owners and high-earning, self-employed individuals to save a large portion of their income for retirement in a tax-advantaged way.

Employer-Only Contributions

In a SEP IRA, contributions are made solely by the employer. Employees do not contribute to the plan themselves. When an employer makes a contribution to a SEP IRA for an employee, the employee receives the contribution into their Traditional IRA, not a separate SEP IRA. While the plan is established as a SEP by the employer, the contributions function as part of the employee's Traditional IRA for tax and investment purposes.

Equal Contributions for All Eligible Employees

A critical requirement of a SEP IRA is that if the employer makes a contribution for themselves, they must also contribute the same percentage of compensation for all eligible employees. This ensures that all employees benefit equally from the plan. Eligibility is generally extended to employees who are at least 21 years old, have worked for the employer at least three of the last five years, and have earned at least $750 in 2024.

Tax Benefits

Contributions made to a SEP IRA are tax deductible for the employer, reducing the business's taxable income for the year. Additionally, the contributions are not included in the employee's gross income, which means that employees benefit from tax-deferred growth on their retirement savings until they take distributions in retirement.

Flexibility for Business Owners

SEP IRAs offer significant flexibility for business owners. There are no annual filing requirements for the employer, and contributions can vary from year to year based on the business's financial situation. This flexibility makes the SEP IRA a great option for businesses with fluctuating profits or those that want to reward employees in profitable years.

BENEFITS OF A SEP IRA

Substantial Retirement Savings Potential

With much higher contribution limits than traditional or Roth IRAs, SEP IRAs allow business owners and self-employed individuals to save a substantial amount for retirement each year. This can be particularly advantageous for those looking to catch up on retirement savings later in their careers or who have a high income and want to take full advantage of tax-deferred growth.

Tax Advantages

Contributions to a SEP IRA are tax-deductible for the business, reducing taxable income. For real estate professionals and other self-employed individuals, this can mean a significant tax break, especially if they are able to contribute a large portion of their income to the SEP IRA.

Easy to Set Up and Administer

Unlike other retirement plans, such as 401(k)s, SEP IRAs are relatively simple to establish and maintain. There are minimal administrative costs and no annual filing requirements with the IRS, making them a low-maintenance option for small businesses.

Ideal for Small Businesses and Self-Employed Individuals

The SEP IRA is particularly well suited for small businesses and self-employed individuals because it offers high contribution limits, tax advantages, and administrative simplicity. It allows these individuals to invest significantly in their own retirement while also providing a valuable benefit to any employees they may have.

CONSIDERATIONS AND LIMITATIONS

Equal Contributions Requirement

One of the most important considerations when establishing a SEP IRA is the requirement to make equal percentage contributions for all eligible employees. While this can be a great benefit for employees, it may be less desirable for business owners who want more flexibility in their contributions or who have a large number of employees, as it can become expensive.

No Employee Contributions

SEP IRAs do not allow employees to contribute to their own retirement savings directly through the plan. For employees who wish to save more for retirement, additional personal savings or a separate retirement account, such as a traditional or Roth IRA, may be necessary.

Consult a Tax Professional

Given the complexity of tax rules and the potential for substantial contributions, it's essential to consult with a tax professional to understand the exact contribution limits and tax implications based on the business's classification, employee status, profits, FICA tax, and tax period. This is particularly important for real estate professionals and others with variable income or complex financial situations.

Potential for High Contributions

Real estate investors and self-employed individuals could potentially fund their SEP IRAs with $69,000 or more each year around tax filing time, which can then be invested in real estate or other assets soon after. This strategy not only accelerates your retirement savings but also provides a significant tax break. Consulting with a tax professional can help you optimize this approach and ensure you're maximizing the benefits of your SEP IRA investment strategy.

SIMPLE IRA

The Savings Incentive Match Plan for Employees (SIMPLE) IRA is a retirement plan designed specifically for small businesses and self-employed individuals. This plan offers a simplified, cost-effective way for employers to provide retirement benefits to their employees, while also allowing business owners to save for their own retirement. Due to its lower administrative costs and straightforward setup compared to other retirement plans, the SIMPLE IRA is an attractive option for sole proprietors, partnerships, and small businesses with a limited number of employees.

WHAT IS A SIMPLE IRA?

A SIMPLE IRA is a type of traditional IRA that allows both employers and employees to contribute to retirement savings. It operates similarly to other employer-sponsored retirement plans, such as a 401(k), but with simpler and more flexible rules. Contributions made to a SIMPLE IRA are tax deferred, meaning that they reduce taxable income in the year they are made and grow tax free until withdrawal.

The SIMPLE IRA is designed for small businesses with one hundred or fewer employees who earned $5,000 or more during the previous calendar year. The plan is especially appealing because it is less expensive and easier to administer than many other types of workplace retirement plans, making it an ideal choice for small businesses looking to offer a retirement benefit without the complexity and cost associated with more comprehensive plans.

KEY FEATURES OF A SIMPLE IRA

Low Administrative Costs

One of the main advantages of a SIMPLE IRA is its low administrative cost. As *CNN Money* notes, "It's cheaper to set up and run a SIMPLE IRA plan than it is to administer many other workplace retirement plans."[25] There are no annual filing requirements with the IRS for employers, and the paperwork associated with establishing and maintaining a SIMPLE IRA is minimal compared to other plans like 401(k)s or profit-sharing plans.

Employer Contribution Options

Employers have flexibility in choosing how they contribute to their employees' SIMPLE IRAs. There are two primary options:

1. Flat 2 percent contribution: Employers can choose to make a nonelective contribution equal to 2 percent of each eligible

---

[25] "Ultimate Guide to Retirement: What Is a SIMPLE IRA," *CNN Money*, accessed September 16, 2024, https://money.cnn.com/retirement/guide/IRA_SIMPLE.moneymag/index.htm.

employee's compensation, regardless of whether the employee contributes to the plan. This contribution is based on the employee's compensation up to $345,000 for 2024.

2. Dollar-for-dollar matching contribution: Employers can match employee contributions on a dollar-for-dollar basis up to 3 percent of the employee's compensation. This matching contribution incentivizes employees to contribute to their retirement savings while providing the employer with flexibility in managing costs.

Employers can reduce the matching contribution to as low as 1 percent in any two out of five years.

As with SEP IRAs, the SECURE 2.0 Act now allows for Roth-type contributions to SIMPLE IRAs. Be sure to discuss your company's SIMPLE contribution strategy with your competent tax advisor.

Employee Contributions

Employees can contribute to their SIMPLE IRA through salary deferrals. For 2024, the contribution limit for employee salary deferrals is $16,000, with an additional catch-up contribution of $3,500 for employees aged 50 or older. These contributions are made on a pretax basis, reducing the employee's taxable income for the year.

Simplicity in Setup and Maintenance

A SIMPLE IRA is easy to set up and maintain, making it an attractive option for small businesses that may not have the resources to manage more complex retirement plans. To establish a SIMPLE IRA, employers need to:

1. Choose a financial institution to serve as the plan's custodian.
2. Complete IRS Form 5304-SIMPLE or 5305-SIMPLE, which serves as the plan's adoption agreement.
3. Provide employees with a summary description of the plan and the required annual notices about their rights and responsibilities.

THE TWO-YEAR RULE

One unique aspect of the SIMPLE IRA is the "two-year rule." This rule states that for the first two years after an employee begins participating in the plan, any distributions or rollovers from the SIMPLE IRA can only be made to another SIMPLE IRA. After this two-year period, funds can be rolled over without triggering taxes to other types of non-Roth IRAs or to an employer-sponsored retirement plan.

- Within the first two years: If you withdraw funds or attempt to roll them over to a traditional IRA, Roth IRA, or another employer-sponsored plan, the distribution is subject to a 25 percent early withdrawal penalty in addition to regular income taxes if you are under the age of 59½.
- After the two-year period: You can roll over funds to any other type of non-Roth IRA or an employer-sponsored retirement plan without incurring the 25 percent penalty. The tax is reduced to 10 percent. Additionally, you can roll over money into a Roth IRA, but any untaxed amounts rolled over must be included in your income for the year, which may result in a higher tax bill.

BENEFITS OF A SIMPLE IRA

Cost-Effectiveness

The SIMPLE IRA is less expensive to set up and maintain than many other types of retirement plans, such as 401(k)s. There are no filing fees with the IRS, and the administrative burden is significantly lower. This cost-effectiveness makes the SIMPLE IRA an appealing choice for small businesses that want to offer retirement benefits without incurring substantial costs.

Tax Advantages

Both employer and employee contributions to a SIMPLE IRA are made with pretax dollars, which can provide significant tax savings. For employers, contributions are tax deductible as a business expense, reducing taxable income. For employees, contributions reduce their taxable income, which can result in lower income taxes in the year of the contribution.

Flexibility for Employers

Employers have the flexibility to choose between a flat contribution rate or a matching program, allowing them to tailor the plan to their financial situation and goals. This flexibility can be particularly beneficial for small businesses with fluctuating revenues or those that want to offer an incentive for employee savings.

Encourages Employee Participation

The matching contribution option encourages employees to participate in the plan and save for their retirement. By providing a dollar-for-dollar match up to 3 percent of compensation, employers can motivate employees to contribute more to their retirement savings, promoting financial security for the future.

CONSIDERATIONS AND LIMITATIONS

Contribution Limits

While the SIMPLE IRA offers higher contribution limits than a traditional IRA, it still has lower limits compared to a 401(k) plan. For businesses with employees who want to save more than the SIMPLE IRA limits allow, a 401(k) or other retirement plan may be a better option.

Early Withdrawal Penalties

The two-year rule imposes a significant penalty on early withdrawals or rollovers to non-SIMPLE IRAs within the first two years of participation. This 25 percent penalty is higher than the 10 percent early withdrawal penalty that typically applies to other types of retirement accounts, making it essential for employees to understand and plan around this rule.

Mandatory Employer Contributions

Unlike other retirement plans where employer contributions may be discretionary, the SIMPLE IRA requires mandatory employer contributions either as a flat 2 percent or a matching contribution up to 3 percent. This requirement could be a disadvantage for businesses that want more flexibility in their contribution levels, especially during periods of low profitability.

Chapter 4

SDIRA Foundations—Other Retirement Accounts

"Self-directed IRAs open up a world of investment possibilities, but they require knowledge and caution. Properly managed, they offer powerful opportunities to build wealth through assets you understand, like real estate and private lending."

—John Hyre, tax attorney and self-directed IRA expert

Employer-sponsored retirement plans such as the 401(k), 403(b), and 457 offer employees powerful tools to save for retirement with tax advantages. These plans are generally designed to help workers set aside a portion of their pretax income and often include employer-matching contributions, further incentivizing savings. Each plan is tailored to specific sectors—401(k)s for private companies, 403(b)s for public schools and nonprofits, and 457s for government employees—but they share common goals of helping employees secure their financial futures. However, these plans typically limit investment options to standard market assets, such as stocks, bonds, and mutual funds, and do not offer self-directed investment options. Understanding these plans is essential for maximizing retirement savings while navigating the rules and opportunities specific to each one.

Employer Plans

The 401(k), 403(b), and 457 plans are all types of employer-sponsored retirement savings plans designed to help employees save for their future. These plans typically do not offer self-directed options to invest outside of the stock market.

A 401(k) plan is the most common and is offered by private sector employers, allowing employees to contribute a portion of their salary before taxes are taken out. Many employers also match a percentage of employee contributions, providing an additional incentive to save. The 403(b) plan is similar to a 401(k) but is specifically available to employees of public schools, nonprofit organizations, and certain other tax-exempt entities. Like the 401(k), the 403(b) allows for pretax contributions and often includes employer matching. The 457 plan is available to employees of state and local governments and some nonprofit organizations. This plan also allows for pretax contributions, but it has different rules regarding withdrawals and contribution limits, especially for those nearing retirement age. Each of these plans provides valuable tax advantages and opportunities for long-term savings tailored to the specific employment sectors they serve.

Borrowing from Your 401(k) Plan—Is It a Good Idea?

While these funds are primarily intended for retirement, there are provisions that allow participants to borrow from their 401(k) accounts for personal use. This flexibility applies not only to employer-based plans but also to solo 401(k)s, making the option available for a broad range of retirement savers. In this section, we'll explore the ins and outs of 401(k) plan loans, including borrowing limits, repayment terms, and the potential risks involved.

WHAT IS A 401(K) PLAN LOAN?

 A 401(k) loan enables plan participants to borrow from their retirement savings rather than withdrawing money and facing taxes and penalties. The borrowed amount must be repaid with interest, but the unique feature of a 401(k) loan is that the interest goes back into the participant's own 401(k) account, not to a lender. This can make the 401(k) loan an appealing option for those who need immediate funds without wanting to tap into other sources, like credit cards or personal loans, which often carry higher interest rates.

Maximum Loan Amount

The IRS sets strict limits on how much you can borrow from your 401(k) to ensure you don't deplete your retirement savings. The maximum loan amount is the lesser of 50 percent of the vested account balance or $50,000.

For example, if your vested account balance is $80,000, you can borrow up to $40,000, which is 50 percent of the balance. However, if your vested account balance is $150,000, the maximum loan you can take is capped at $50,000, not 50 percent of $150,000.

The term "vested" refers to the portion of your retirement account that you fully own and cannot be taken back by your employer. Some employers may require you to work a certain number of years before you are fully vested in their contributions to your 401(k), but your personal contributions are always 100 percent vested.

Repayment Terms

Once you borrow from your 401(k), the loan must be repaid within a maximum of five years. The repayments must be made in substantially equal installments that include both principal and interest, and they must be made at least quarterly. It's important to note that these loan repayments are not considered plan contributions, so they don't benefit from the tax advantages of regular 401(k) contributions.

If you're using the loan to purchase a primary residence, the repayment term can extend beyond five years, depending on your plan's provisions.

Interest Rates

The interest rate on a 401(k) loan is generally set by the plan administrator, and it typically follows the prime rate, with an additional 1 or 2 percent. While the interest rate may vary, it is generally lower than the rates you would pay on a personal loan or a credit card.

One key advantage of a 401(k) loan is that the interest you pay goes back into your own account, so you are essentially paying yourself to borrow the money. This is in stark contrast to conventional loans, where interest payments go to a lender.

Pros and Cons of 401(k) Loans

Pros:
- ✓ **No credit check:** Because you're borrowing from your own retirement savings, there's no need for a credit check or approval process. This makes a 401(k) loan an accessible option for those with less-than-ideal credit.
- ✓ **Low interest rates:** Compared to other forms of borrowing like personal loans or credit cards, the interest rates on 401(k) loans are generally lower, which can save you money in the long run.
- ✓ **Repayment to yourself:** Unlike traditional loans, where interest goes to a lender, the interest on a 401(k) loan is credited back to your own retirement account.

Cons:

- × **Repayment is required:** If you fail to repay the loan on time, the remaining balance is treated as a distribution. This means you'll owe income taxes on the amount, and if you're under the age of 59½, you'll likely face a 10 percent early withdrawal penalty.
- × **Opportunity cost:** While you have an outstanding loan, the money you've borrowed is no longer invested in your 401(k), meaning it's not growing or compounding tax deferred. This can result in a lower retirement balance than if the funds had remained invested.
- × **Job loss risk:** If you leave your job, whether voluntarily or involuntarily, you'll be required to repay the loan in full by the tax filing deadline for that year, including any extensions. If you can't repay the loan in time, the remaining balance is treated as a taxable distribution, which could lead to a significant tax bill.

Important Considerations

Before taking a 401(k) loan, it's essential to evaluate your overall financial situation. A 401(k) loan may provide quick access to funds, but it's important to consider the long-term impact on your retirement savings. Keep in mind that borrowing from your 401(k) means you're temporarily reducing the amount of money invested for your retirement, which could have serious consequences later in life.

Also, a 401(k) loan should be viewed as a short-term solution. While it can help with immediate cash flow needs, relying on your retirement savings to cover personal expenses can set back your progress toward a secure retirement.

It's wise to explore other options before borrowing from your 401(k). Could you use savings or take out a low-interest personal loan? Would it be better to adjust your budget temporarily instead of borrowing from your future retirement?

IRS Guidelines on 401(k) Loans

The IRS provides clear guidelines on the rules and regulations surrounding 401(k) loans, including how much you can borrow, repayment terms, and what happens if you default. Be sure to review these guidelines or consult with a financial advisor to ensure you fully understand the implications of borrowing from your 401(k).

Borrowing from your employer plan can be a useful financial tool in times of need, offering flexibility and access to funds without immediate tax penalties. However, it's important to fully understand the terms of the loan, the repayment obligations, and the potential impact on your long-term retirement savings. Always consider the pros and cons carefully, and consult with a financial advisor to determine if this option aligns with your financial goals.

While a 401(k) loan can help you manage short-term financial needs, it comes with risks. The decision to borrow from your 401(k) should not be made lightly, as it may affect your ability to retire comfortably.

Utilizing the Health Savings Account (HSA) as a Self-Directed Savings Vehicle: A Tax-Free Strategy for 2024

Health savings accounts (HSAs) are often thought of solely as a way to pay for medical expenses with pretax dollars, but savvy investors are increasingly recognizing their value as a powerful tool for long-term, tax-advantaged savings. As we look ahead to 2024, the changes in contribution limits and the continued flexibility of HSAs make them even more attractive for those who wish to self-direct their savings and maximize tax-free growth.

WHAT IS AN HSA?

An HSA is tied to your high-deductible health insurance plan at work. Moreover, an HSA is a tax-advantaged savings account designed to help individuals save for qualified medical expenses. To be eligible, you must be enrolled in a high-deductible health plan (HDHP). The real magic of the HSA lies in its triple tax advantage: contributions are made pretax (or tax-deductible), the money grows tax-free, and withdrawals for qualified medical expenses are tax-free. This makes the HSA one of the most tax-efficient savings vehicles available today.

CHANGES IN 2024: HIGHER CONTRIBUTION LIMITS

Starting in 2024, the maximum HSA contribution limits increased to $4,150 for individuals and $8,300 for families, with an additional $1,000 catch-up contribution available for those 55 and older. This is a jump from the 2023 limits of $3,850 for individuals and $7,750 for families, providing more room for tax-advantaged growth.

HSA AS A SELF-DIRECTED SAVINGS VEHICLE

One of the underutilized features of the HSA is its potential as a self-directed investment account. Just like a self-directed IRA, a self-directed HSA allows you to invest in a wide variety of asset classes, including stocks, bonds, mutual funds, and even more alternative investments like real estate, provided the HSA provider supports it. By strategically investing your HSA funds, you can grow your savings over time while enjoying the tax-free benefits that come with the account.

The flexibility of the HSA extends beyond just paying for immediate medical expenses. Many investors use their HSA to grow funds tax free and only tap into the account for qualified medical expenses later in retirement when health care costs are likely to rise. You can pay out of pocket for current medical expenses and allow the HSA to continue growing, taking advantage of compounding tax-free growth.

THE TRIPLE TAX ADVANTAGE: HOW IT WORKS

1. Pretax contributions: Any contributions you make to your HSA are either pretax (if made through payroll deductions) or tax deductible, meaning they lower your taxable income for the year.
2. Tax-free growth: As long as the money remains in the account, any investment earnings grow tax free. This is especially beneficial when using a self-directed HSA to invest in higher-growth options like stocks or mutual funds.
3. Tax-free withdrawal: When you withdraw money from your HSA for qualified medical expenses, those withdrawals are entirely tax free. There's no other savings vehicle that offers this level of tax advantage.

LONG-TERM BENEFITS: HSAs AND RETIREMENT PLANNING

HSAs can also serve as a stealth retirement savings tool. After age 65, you can use the funds in your HSA for nonmedical expenses, though withdrawals for these purposes will be taxed as ordinary income, like a traditional IRA or 401(k). However, when you use the funds for qualified medical expenses, they remain tax free, which is a considerable advantage since health care costs tend to increase as you age.

By investing in your HSA and letting it grow over time, you can potentially accumulate a significant amount of tax-free money that can be used to cover major health care costs in retirement, such as Medicare premiums, long-term care, or out-of-pocket expenses. The 2024 increase in contribution limits allows you to save even more, maximizing the growth potential.

WHO BENEFITS FROM USING AN HSA AS A SELF-DIRECTED SAVINGS VEHICLE?

High-income individuals, savvy investors, and those looking to optimize their retirement savings can particularly benefit from utilizing an HSA as a self-directed savings vehicle. If you're in a high tax bracket, the pretax contributions and tax-free growth can help you lower your current taxable income while building a substantial nest egg for future health care costs. Additionally, those who are already maximizing their 401(k) or IRA contributions can use an HSA as an additional savings vehicle with significant tax benefits.

MAIN POINTS:

- Maximize contributions: In 2024, take full advantage of the increased HSA contribution limits—$4,150 for individuals and $8,300 for families, with an additional $1,000 for those 55 and older.
- Triple tax advantage: Contributions, growth, and qualified withdrawals are all tax free, making the HSA one of the most tax-efficient accounts available.
- Self-directed options: You can invest your HSA funds in a wide range of asset classes, allowing for greater growth potential.
- Long-term strategy: Let your HSA grow by paying out of pocket for medical expenses now, then reimbursing yourself later in retirement while enjoying tax-free growth.

The HSA is not just a tool for covering medical expenses—it's a versatile and powerful vehicle for long-term, tax-free savings. If you're not utilizing it to its full potential, especially with the 2024 changes, it's time to rethink your strategy and explore how a self-directed HSA could fit into your broader financial and retirement planning.

THE SELF-DIRECTED EDUCATION SAVINGS ACCOUNT

A Self-Directed Coverdell Education Savings Account (ESA) is a tax-advantaged savings vehicle designed to help families save for education expenses, with the added benefit of allowing a wide range of investment options. Unlike traditional Coverdell ESAs, which may restrict investment choices to typical options like stocks, bonds, and mutual funds, a self-directed ESA provides more flexibility. Investors can choose to invest in a broader array of asset classes, including real estate, private equity, and even precious metals, similar to an SDIRA. This increased flexibility allows individuals to potentially grow their education savings more aggressively, depending on their risk tolerance and investment strategy.

The tax advantages of a Coverdell ESA are significant. Contributions to the account grow tax-deferred, meaning that earnings accumulate without being subject to taxes each year. Moreover, when funds are withdrawn for qualified education expenses, such as tuition, books, or even K-12 costs, those withdrawals are entirely tax-free. However, there are limitations: the annual contribution limit for a Coverdell ESA is $2,000 per beneficiary, and contributions must be made before the beneficiary turns 18 (unless they have special needs). The account must also be used by the time the beneficiary turns 30, or the remaining balance may be subject to taxes and penalties. A self-directed Coverdell ESA can be a powerful tool for families looking to take a more active role in managing their education savings, especially if they seek higher returns through alternative investments.

Retirement Account Requirements for Minors

A minor child can contribute to a retirement account, such as an IRA, as long as they have earned income, regardless of their age. "Earned income" refers to taxable compensation from activities such as wages, salaries, tips, or self-employment income. The key requirement is that the child must actually be earning income, but there are no age limits preventing them from contributing to either a traditional or Roth IRA. Parents or guardians typically set up the IRA as a custodial account, which means the adult manages the account until the child reaches the age of majority, but the account is still in the child's name and for their benefit.

For example, a child might earn income by working part time, babysitting, or helping with a family business. As long as that income is properly documented, either through a W-2 or 1099 form, the child can contribute up to the lesser of their earned income or the annual contribution limit for the IRA ($7,000 for 2024). If the child doesn't have enough to contribute on their own, parents or other family members can contribute on their behalf, as long as the contributions do not exceed the child's earned income for the year. This is a powerful tool to start saving early, allowing the child's retirement funds to benefit from decades of compound growth.

Parents or guardians who own a business can also hire their children to perform work, such as office tasks, cleaning, or helping with other age-appropriate tasks. The compensation must be reasonable, given the child's age and experience level, but doing so provides the dual benefit of teaching the child about work and responsibility while also creating an opportunity for early retirement savings. These contributions grow tax free within the IRA, offering the child a head start on building a substantial retirement nest egg.

Chapter 5

Tax Benefits of SDIRAs

"Retirement accounts are some of our most valuable
financial tools. With the ability to grow investments tax
deferred or tax free, they give us a powerful advantage
in accelerating wealth-building."

—Amanda Han, Keystone CPA, coauthor of *The Book on Tax Strategies
for the Savvy Real Estate Investor*

SDIRAs offer a variety of tax advantages that make them an attractive option for investors looking to grow their retirement savings.
One of the primary benefits of an SDIRA is tax-deferred growth. This
means that the investments within the account, such as foreign curren-
cies or other asset classes, grow without being subject to immediate
taxation. Instead, taxes are deferred until the funds are distributed
during retirement, allowing the investments to compound over time
without the drag of annual taxes. This can result in significant growth
of the retirement account compared to taxable investment accounts.

Another significant advantage is the potential for tax-free returns.
When income, profit, or appreciation from investments in an SDIRA
are realized, they are returned directly to the account without being
taxed or contributing to the account holder's taxable income. For
example, if an investor uses an SDIRA to purchase a property, make
renovations, and then sell it for a profit, the proceeds from the sale
go back into the SDIRA without incurring immediate taxes. This can
provide a substantial tax saving compared to using personal funds for
the investment, where profits would be subject to capital gains tax.

SDIRAs also offer the benefit of diversification, allowing investors
to spread their investments across a wide range of asset types beyond
traditional stocks and bonds. These include real estate, private equity,
precious metals, and even oil and gas projects. By diversifying their
portfolios, investors can reduce risk and potentially create multiple
streams of income, enhancing both the growth and stability of their
retirement savings.

Beyond these tax advantages, SDIRAs can offer other benefits.
For instance, using an SDIRA to purchase a multifamily property

not only provides potential tax savings and income but also offers various exit strategies, such as selling, refinancing, or improving the property. This flexibility can be particularly beneficial in uncertain economic times as it allows the investor to adapt to changing conditions. Furthermore, SDIRAs give account holders complete control over their investment decisions, empowering them to tailor their portfolios according to their own strategies and risk tolerance. This level of control can be appealing to experienced investors who prefer to actively manage their retirement funds.

Overall, the tax advantages and investment flexibility offered by SDIRAs make them a powerful tool for building and protecting retirement wealth.

What Can SDIRAs Invest In?

SDIRAs open the door to investing in a wide range of investments with many diverse strategies and tactics for a truly well-rounded and optimized portfolio.

ALLOWABLE INVESTMENTS INCLUDE:

- Residential real estate
- Commercial real estate
- Undeveloped or raw land
- REITs (real estate investment trusts)
- Real estate notes (mortgages and deeds of trusts)
- Promissory notes
- Private limited partnerships
- Limited liability companies
- Cryptocurrency
- C corporations
- Tax lien certificates
- Oil and gas investments
- Private stock offerings/private placements
- Judgments/structured settlements
- Gold bullion
- Car paper
- Factoring investments
- Accounts receivables
- Equipment leasing

Real estate–specific assets permitted include:

- Single-family homes
- Two- to four-unit multifamily properties
- Apartment buildings
- Townhomes
- Condominiums
- Vacant land and lots
- Mobile and manufactured homes/parks
- Mortgage debt
- Real estate businesses and start-ups
- Office buildings
- Retail properties
- Industrial and warehouse property
- Mixed-use properties

Real estate investment strategies and vehicles that are permitted in SDIRAs:

- ✓ Shares and stock of real estate companies
- ✓ Interests in real estate limited liability companies (LLCs) and real estate limited partnerships (LPs)
- ✓ REITs (real estate investment trusts)
- ✓ Property rights (air, timber, oil and gas, etc.)
- ✓ Buying and holding income property
- ✓ Fixing and flipping real estate
- ✓ Wholesaling houses
- ✓ New construction

What cannot be invested in using an SDIRA (prohibited investments):

- ✕ Shares of S corporations
- ✕ Most types of collectibles
- ✕ Artwork
- ✕ Life insurance contracts
- ✕ Property acquired for personal use
- ✕ Property to be used by disqualified persons

Limitations and Prohibited Transactions

There are three pitfalls that are important to watch for in SDIRA investments:

1. Prohibited investments
2. Prohibited transactions
3. Triggering UBIT/ UDFI tax liability

The IRS itself does not approve investments; it only dictates what IRAs cannot invest in and what types of specific transactions may disqualify the IRA and account owner from tax protections.

From time to time, the IRS will issue letters to IRA sponsors, trustees, and custodians to certify that they are in compliance with requirements, administration standards, and documentation that allow contributions to be deductible.

The IRA owner can stay protected by avoiding the above list of prohibited investments and by understanding prohibited transactions.

There are two main parts to this:

1. Comingling of personal funds and SDIRA assets
2. Disqualified persons becoming involved in IRA transactions

Examples of prohibited transactions include:

- Borrowing money from one's own IRA
- Selling one's own property to the IRA
- Personal use of property held by one's own IRA
- Pledging an IRA as collateral for a loan
- Receiving income compensation for managing one's own IRA assets

Disqualified persons cannot buy, sell, rent, or do business with one's own IRA. These persons may include the owner's:

- Client (a fiduciary is a disallowed person)
- Spouse
- Parents
- Natural grandparents
- Stepchildren

- Natural children
- Grandchildren
- IRA service providers
- Beneficiaries, trustees, and IRA administrators
- 50/50 business partners

The topic of prohibited transactions and the ability to self-direct and manage real estate investments continues to cause confusion for SDIRA account holders. It is wise to consult your administrator-custodian in advance, create a plan, and keep an eye on emerging legal cases and rulings.

Understanding UBIT and UDFI Taxes

When investing through an SDIRA, it's essential for investors to be aware of certain taxes that can apply to their investments, particularly the unrelated business income tax (UBIT) and unrelated debt-financed income (UDFI) tax. Both taxes are outlined in IRS Publication 598 and can significantly impact the returns on investments held within an SDIRA.

Unrelated business income tax (UBIT) applies to income generated from a business activity that is not substantially related to the tax-exempt purpose of the IRA. This means that if an SDIRA owns an interest in a business, such as a limited liability company (LLC) or partnership that generates active income (i.e., income from the operation of a business), that income could be subject to UBIT. The purpose of UBIT is to level the playing field between tax-exempt entities and taxable businesses by taxing the income that does not relate directly to the IRA's primary purpose of passive investment growth.

Unrelated debt-financed income (UDFI) tax, on the other hand, applies when an SDIRA acquires investment property with borrowed funds. When an SDIRA uses debt to finance an investment, such as purchasing real estate with a mortgage, the income attributable to the financed portion of the investment is subject to UDFI tax. The idea here is to prevent tax-exempt entities from gaining an unfair advantage by using leverage to increase their returns without being subject to taxation. The UDFI tax is calculated based on the ratio of the debt to the property's acquisition price and applies to the income generated by that investment.

For self-directed investors, the impact of UBIT and UDFI can be substantial. These taxes can reduce the overall return on investments held within an SDIRA and add complexity to the tax reporting requirements. Investors need to be aware of the types of investments that may trigger these taxes and consider the potential tax liability when evaluating investment opportunities. It's advisable to consult with a tax professional familiar with SDIRA rules and IRS regulations to understand fully how UBIT and UDFI may affect their investment strategy and ensure compliance with tax laws.

How Investments Are Made Through SDIRAs

The most common, and arguably the safest, most prosperous, way for individuals to execute investments and transactions through an SDIRA is to instruct the account administrator to make the desired investment transaction. Every administrator will have its own procedures for this. Here is one scenario:

- Jane Doe decides she wants her SDIRA to invest in a rental property in Texas.
- Jane instructs her administrator to make the investment on her behalf from the IRA's funds.
- The administration reviews the documents to ensure compliance and writes the check.
- The check, wire, or ACH is sent as Jane indicates.
- The asset posts to Jane's account as an asset of the plan.
- Proceeds from the asset post to the general ledger of Jane's account.

Making an investment through an SDIRA is simple, yet there need to be checks in place. Making a misstep can create financial and tax issues. It pays to ensure that the account holder (i.e., you) has double-checked everything. It is the IRA owner's responsibility to understand the rules, and the administrator is there to provide that education.

Chapter 6

How Much Money Can Be Invested in IRAs?

"What's really nice is that the IRS doesn't tell us what we can invest in, only what we can't do. So it's a short list."

When it comes to investing in IRAs, the possibilities are nearly limitless. While the IRS provides guidelines on what you cannot invest in, the range of acceptable investments remains vast, allowing savvy investors to leverage their assets in diverse ways. This chapter explores how much money can be invested in IRAs and the potential for maximizing those funds through strategic investment choices. With trillions of dollars in American retirement accounts waiting to be tapped, understanding how to unlock this pool of capital is crucial for real estate professionals and anyone looking to diversify their investment portfolio beyond traditional options. Let's dive into the numbers and see just how much financial power is at your fingertips

How much money can individuals invest through their IRAs? How can they gain leverage and maximize that figure?

More than All the Gold in Fort Knox

According to the U.S. Treasury Department, the United States Bullion Depository, commonly known as Fort Knox, holds an estimated 143.7 million ounces of the United States' gold reserves as of March 2024.[26] That's worth an approximate $518 billion.

How much is in American retirement accounts?

At the end of September 2024, the Investment Company Institute (ICI) reported U.S. retirement assets had risen to $40.0 trillion.[27] That translates to around 32 percent of all national household financial assets. IRAs made up the bulk of these funds, at $14.5 trillion. The rest

---

[26] "Does Fort Knox Still Have Gold?" Garfield Refining, March 22, 2024, https://www.garfieldre-fining.com/resources/blog/does-fort-knox-still-have-gold/.

[27] "Release: Quarterly Retirement Market Data," ICI: Investment Company Institute," September 19, 2024, https://www.ici.org/statistical-report/ret_24_q2.

is split between private sector and government-defined contribution and defined benefit plans, including 401(k) plans.[28]

IRA and 401(k) plan assets alone dwarf the world's largest gold reserves. Yet few individuals know what those dollars are really invested in or how much they are paying in fees.

This stark contrast between the vast wealth stored in retirement accounts and the limited awareness of their actual investments underscores the importance of understanding where money is allocated and how it performs. To put this into perspective, examining significant trends in real estate and market values provides a tangible example of the scale and impact of investment opportunities available today.

Here are some updated insights on significant real estate and market value trends from recent years:

- New York City's property value: As of 2024, New York City's total property market value increased to $1.49 trillion, showing consistent growth from earlier years despite market fluctuations. This represents a 0.7 percent increase from 2023, reflecting the city's robust recovery patterns across different property classes, particularly in commercial real estate.[29]
- U.S. residential real estate: Zillow estimated the total value of U.S. homes had reached $43.4 trillion by 2023, reflecting continued substantial growth since 2020. This is a significant increase from prior years, driven by rising home prices and housing demand.[30]
- Global commercial real estate: Global commercial real estate values have continued to rise, with expectations for stronger performance toward the second half of the year 2024.[31] The overall value of global real estate was estimated

[28] *U.S. Retirement Assets: Data in Brief,* Congressional Research Service, September 20, 2023, https://crsreports.congress.gov/product/pdf/R/R47699.

[29] "Department of Finance Publishes Fiscal Year 2025 Tentative Property Tax Assessment Roll," NYC Department of Finance, January 16, 2024, https://www.nyc.gov/site/finance/about/press/press-release-fy25-tentative-assessment-roll.page.

[30] "Understand Market Behavior: Research and Statistics," NAR: National Association of Realtors, accessed September 23, 2024, https://www.nar.realtor/research-and-statistics.

[31] "Global Real Estate Outlook 2024," *JLL,* accessed September 23, 2024, https://www.us.jll.com/en/trends-and-insights/research/global/global-real-estate-outlook.

at approximately $379.9 trillion at the end of 2022,[32] and while certain sectors face challenges, particularly office spaces, segments like logistics and residential remain strong growth areas.[33]

- Stock market value changes: The COVID-19 pandemic saw unprecedented volatility in global markets. In March 2020, U.S. stock markets lost around $11 trillion in value within weeks, echoing the market correction in early 2016. However, recovery across real estate markets has generally outpaced other asset classes in subsequent years.[34]

- U.S. commercial real estate: By the end of 2023, the value of U.S. commercial real estate had reached $647 billion.[35] Despite the. challenges posed by the pandemic, sectors like multifamily housing and industrial real estate saw strong demand.[36]

These trends highlight the resilience and continued appeal of real estate investments in both residential and commercial sectors, driven by factors like economic recovery, market stability, and rising property values. This continued growth positions real estate as a key asset class for both institutional and individual investors looking for stable, long-term returns.

How much can Americans put into their retirement funds and roll over into real estate investments? Here's where we need to talk about the contribution limits.

---

[32] Paul Tostevin and Charlotte Rushton, "Total Value of Global Real Estate: Property Remains the World's Biggest Store of Wealth," *Savills*, September 2023, https://www.savills.com/impacts/market-trends/the-total-value-of-global-real-estate-property-remains-the-worlds-biggest-store-of-wealth.html.

[33] "Global Real Estate Outlook 2024." *JLL*, accessed September 23, 2024, https://www.us.jll.com/en/trends-and-insights/research/global/global-real-estate-outlook.

[34] "Global Real Estate Outlook 2024."

[35] Jack Caporal, "Commercial Real Estate Investing Statistics for 2024," *The Motley Fool*, June 28, 2024, https://www.fool.com/research/commercial-real-estate-investing-statistics/

[36] "Department of Finance Publishes Fiscal Year 2025 Tentative Property Tax Assessment Roll," NYC Department of Finance, January 16, 2024, https://www.nyc.gov/site/finance/about/press/press-release-fy25-tentative-assessment-roll.page.

Contribution Limits

As of 2025, standard annual contribution limits per individual were:

- **Traditional IRAs:** $7,000 ($8,000 for those 50 plus)
- **Roth IRAs:** $7,000 ($8,000 for those 50 plus)
- **401(k)s:** $23,500 ($31,000 for those 50 plus)[37]
- **Solo 401(k):** The total contribution to a solo 401(k) is the lesser of 25 percent of your income up to a cap of $70,000.

There is also a Saver's Tax Credit, also known as the Retirement Savings Contributions Credit, which is a tax incentive designed to encourage low- to moderate-income individuals to save for retirement. This credit allows eligible taxpayers to reduce their federal income tax liability by a percentage of their contributions to qualifying retirement accounts, such as traditional or Roth IRAs, 401(k) plans, and certain other retirement plans.

Here's how the Saver's Tax Credit works:

- Eligibility: To qualify for the Saver's Tax Credit, you must be at least 18 years old, not a full-time student, and not claimed as a dependent on another person's tax return. Your adjusted gross income (AGI) must also be below certain thresholds. For 2024, the credit is available to single filers with an AGI of up to $38,250, head-of-household filers with an AGI of up to $57,375, and married couples filing jointly with an AGI of up to $76,500.
- Credit amount: The credit amount is a percentage of the contributions made to qualifying retirement accounts. The percentage ranges from 10 percent to 50 percent, depending on your filing status and AGI. The maximum contribution eligible for the credit is $2,000 for single filers and $4,000 for married couples filing jointly. Thus, the maximum credit amount can be up to $1,000 for single filers and $2,000 for married couples.
- Contribution limits: The Saver's Tax Credit is separate from the maximum contribution limits set by the IRS for retirement accounts. Individuals can contribute up to these

---

[37] "401(k) Limit Increases to $23,500 for 2025, IRA limit remains $7,000," Internal Revenue Service, November 1, 2024, https://www.irs.gov/newsroom/401k-limit-increases-to-23500-for-2025-ira-limit-remains-7000.

limits and still be eligible for the credit as long as they meet the income requirements.

- Impact for self-employed individuals: Self-employed business owners have additional opportunities to contribute more significantly to retirement plans, especially if they use SEP IRAs, SIMPLE IRAs, or solo 401(k) plans. These plans have higher contribution limits than traditional IRAs, allowing self-employed individuals to save tens of thousands of dollars annually, which can potentially qualify for the Saver's Tax Credit, depending on their income and other factors.

The Saver's Tax Credit is a valuable incentive for those who qualify, offering a direct reduction in tax liability in addition to the benefits of saving for retirement.[38]

Rolling over to a Self-Directed IRA

While standard annual contributions may not sound like a lot, they can add up quickly. A couple contributing a combined $11,000 per year to their retirement accounts—and earning a modest 10 percent annual return—can balloon their retirement savings to over $2,000,000 in thirty years. With the average existing retirement account balance sitting at around $100,000, many have a substantial nest egg with which to begin investing in real estate.

Those with existing 401(k) and IRA plans may not be able to transfer or rollover to self-directed plans until they leave the service of their current employer. It is possible to ask the current 401(k) plan administrator if an "in-service transfer" is available. An "in-service transfer" provision may appear in the 401(k)'s plan document. If so, funds from an existing employer can be rolled over.

For those with 401(k) plans from previous employers, this is a relatively easy process. Simply complete the rollover documentation from the 401(k) administrator and begin the process.

---

[38] "Saver's Credit Can Help Low- and Moderate-Income Taxpayers to Save More in 2024," Internal Revenue Service, November 22, 2023, https://www.irs.gov/newsroom/savers-credit-can-help-low-and-moderate-income-taxpayers-to-save-more-in-2024.

This is a relatively easy process. For transfers from existing IRAs, the new custodian will provide the account holder with the necessary form to complete. For existing 401(k) and 403(b) accounts, current custodians will typically provide the form to request and facilitate the move. This process may take a couple of weeks from the start to when the funds clear with the new custodian.

Leveraging Retirement Funds to Grow a Portfolio

Due to the amount of capital they have in their retirement accounts, some individuals may feel discouraged about investing in real estate. They feel like they don't have enough money to invest. This isn't necessarily true, because there are different ways to augment this investable capital with leverage—for example, with nonrecourse loans or partnerships.

Nonrecourse loans are a specific type of financing option available to retirement accounts, such as SDIRAs, that invest in assets like real estate. Unlike traditional loans, nonrecourse loans do not hold the borrower personally liable. Instead, the loan is secured solely by the property being purchased. If the borrower defaults, the lender can only seize the property used as collateral; they cannot pursue the borrower's other personal assets or the remaining balance in the retirement account. This structure is particularly important for retirement accounts due to the IRS rules prohibiting personal guarantees on loans for retirement investments. Nonrecourse loans enable retirement accounts to leverage their assets without risking additional penalties or disqualification, providing a powerful tool for growing retirement savings through investment while maintaining compliance with IRS regulations.

An IRA cannot be made liable for a debt. An IRA cannot take out mortgages or loans in the traditional sense. However, IRA funds can be used in tandem with nonrecourse loans—those that do not require personal or corporate guarantees. There is no recourse in the case of a default beyond the property being foreclosed.

For this reason, nonrecourse loans typically have lower loan-to-value (LTV) ratios. Rates can be good, but LTVs can often be limited to around 50–70 percent, depending on the current market. Still, this offers the ability to double the size of investments.

Let's say you are the IRA account holder. You might couple a $100,000 retirement fund with a $100,000 nonrecourse loan to purchase and generate income from a $200,000 property.

An IRA can also be leveraged within a partnership structure. In partnerships, investors can pool their resources, combining financial capital, expertise, and connections to undertake larger projects than they could manage individually. Partnerships allow investors to share the risks and rewards of an investment, making it easier to finance significant ventures like real estate developments, business acquisitions, or other high-value investments. Additionally, partnerships often attract more capital because they offer potential investors a structured and diversified opportunity, thereby appealing to a broader range of funding sources. This collaboration can also provide investors with access to new markets, specialized knowledge, and a wider network, enhancing the overall success and profitability of the investment. In essence, partnerships enable investors to leverage their collective strengths, increase their capital base, and achieve financial goals that might be out of reach when working alone.

In a partnership structure, let's say you put in $100,000 for a 10 percent stake in a $1 million multifamily apartment building, mixed-use property (a property used for both commercial and residential purposes), or retail strip mall. If the entity acquiring the commercial asset uses 50 percent nonrecourse financing, that gives the individual investor a stake in a $2 million property, which may have lower per-unit costs and better upside potential. In other words, it may be a great investment.

An IRA can also be leveraged within a partnership structure. In this scenario, let's say you put in $100,000 for a 10 percent stake in a $1 million multifamily apartment building, mixed-use property (a property used for both commercial and residential purposes), or retail strip mall. If the entity acquiring the commercial asset uses 50 percent nonrecourse financing, that gives the individual investor a stake in a $2 million property, which may have lower per-unit costs and better upside potential. In other words, it may be a great investment.

Because of the leverage provided by the nonrecourse loan, your original $100,000 investment now represents a 10 percent stake in a $2 million property, not just a $1 million one. This effectively doubles the value of the property your investment could buy without requiring additional capital from you. As a result, your investment could benefit from potentially higher returns due to the larger property size, lower per-unit costs, and increased upside potential if the property appreciates in value or generates strong rental income.

While this method is hotly debated and brings more risk of crossing the line of prohibited transactions, it can be argued that recent legal cases support being able to collaborate with one's own IRA in a real estate investment.

CAN YOU PARTNER WITH AN IRA IN AN INVESTMENT?

Yes, it is technically possible to partner with your SDIRA in certain instances (though, it is not always worth it to do so. More on this later.). For example, you can partner your SDIRA funds with anyone, including yourself and other disqualified persons, as long as the transaction is new. This means that even spouses or other disqualified persons can partner their IRAs to purchase an investment property if it's a new transaction.

However, you must tread very carefully when doing so. Mixing personal and IRA funds increases the risk of audit and penalties. A notable example is the case of Kellerman v. Rice, where the Kellermans used both personal and IRA assets to invest in real estate. Their investment aimed to develop adjoining parcels of land, but because the transaction benefitted both the Kellermans personally and their IRA, it was deemed a prohibited transaction. The key issue was that the IRA was not the sole beneficiary of the investment, which violates IRS rules.[39]

THE LEGAL DEBATE AROUND PARTNERING WITH YOUR IRA

While partnering with your IRA is a debated topic, recent legal cases suggest that it is possible to collaborate with your IRA in certain investments, but the risk remains high.

However, the case of Rollins v. Commissioner highlights the risks involved. In this case, the account holder invested IRA funds into an entity in which he had a 6 percent personal ownership interest. The IRS found that the transaction violated the indirect benefit rules, which prohibit transactions that result in personal gain for the account holder

---

[39] Read more about the Kellerman case at https://casetext.com/case/kellerman-v-rice-in-re-kellerman-1.

or other disqualified persons. The IRS imposed significant fines due to this prohibited transaction.[40]

Additionally, the Department of Labor (DOL) ruling 2006-1A extended the potential for a negative finding on such activities. It determined that any transaction where the purpose is to benefit a disqualified person could be deemed prohibited.[41]

Even if your argument is "I have the money, but I want my IRA to participate," the problem persists. The IRS can argue that the IRA's involvement in the transaction helps keep the investment healthy and profitable, which provides a personal benefit. The burden of proof then shifts to the taxpayer to show that no personal benefit occurred, which is difficult and risky.

IS IT WORTH IT?

In general, the answer is no. Partnering personal and IRA funds is often not worth the risk. The IRS scrutinizes these types of transactions heavily, and the consequences of getting it wrong can be severe. Even if you believe the transaction is structured correctly, the risk of an audit or penalties remains high. The rules under IRC Section 4975 are very clear about avoiding the commingling of personal and IRA funds. If violated, the entire IRA could be disqualified, leading to immediate distribution of all assets, triggering taxes and penalties.[42]

MAIN POINTS:

- **Prohibited transactions:** According to IRC Section 4975, certain types of transactions between an IRA and disqualified persons are strictly prohibited. These include any actions where personal funds are commingled with IRA funds.
- **Indirect benefits:** The IRS indirect benefit rules prohibit transactions that result in personal gain for the account holder, even if the benefit is indirect. This includes the scenario where an IRA investment indirectly benefits you by keeping the overall investment profitable.

---

[40] Learn more about the Rollins case at https://www.irs.gov/charities-non-profits/private-foundations-amount-involved-self-dealing-lending-of-money-to-disqualified-persons-irc-section-4941e2.

[41] Read more about the DOL ruling 2006-1A at https://www.dol.gov/agencies/ebsa/about-ebsa/our-activities/resource-center/advisory-opinions/2006-01a.

[42] Review IRC Section 4975 at https://www.law.cornell.edu/uscode/text/26/4975.

- **Audits and penalties:** If the IRS finds that personal and IRA funds are improperly mixed, it can disqualify the IRA, leading to taxes and penalties that could seriously harm your retirement savings.

While it's technically possible to partner with your IRA on an investment, the risks often outweigh the benefits due to the IRS's stringent rules on prohibited transactions and indirect benefits. Structuring such deals in compliance with these regulations can be challenging, and even if executed correctly, the IRS may scrutinize the transaction closely, making this a potentially risky strategy.

A viable alternative is to use non-recourse loans, which can be utilized either by the IRA alone or as part of a partnership arrangement. These strategies offer flexibility and can even be used together, providing opportunities to diversify and expand investment potential while remaining compliant with IRS rules. Additionally, employing the non-recourse loan strategy solely within an SDIRA—without entering into a partnership—simplifies the structure and minimizes risk.

In practical terms, real estate investments often come with bills, such as property taxes. Taxing authorities typically do not accept partial payments from multiple parties, such as one from an IRA and another from a partner. Instead, they require a single payment for the entire amount.

One solution we've seen is for the non-IRA partner to create an LLC, with the IRA investing in that LLC. This structure allows the LLC to handle payments, such as property taxes, with a single check, reducing potential complications.

If you're considering any of these strategies, it's essential to consult with a qualified tax specialist or attorney experienced in IRA regulations. While non-recourse loans and partnership arrangements can provide viable investment options, they require careful planning to avoid prohibited transactions and ensure compliance with the law.

Chapter 7

Understanding the Rules

"The IRS has something called the indirect rule where if you can't do it directly, you can't do it indirectly."

The IRS doesn't come right out and say what can be invested in using the SDIRA. However, if something is invested in using the SDIRA that is not allowed by the IRS, they will let the account holder know, and it's not always pretty. Before using one's SDIRA for investment purposes, one must get familiar with the term "administratively feasible." The term is intentionally vague, but it typically describes an asset the custodian will hold. For example, if someone came to us to invest their SDIRA funds to acquire a racehorse, we would tell them that asset is not administratively feasible. It is not an asset we choose to hold in custody.

At uDirect, this is typically the first question we ask when a prospective account holder comes to us to start the SDIRA process: What are you looking to invest in? If the investment comes with questionable concerns, then it may not be feasible for the custodian to hold.

Next, there are life insurance contracts and collectibles to consider. As I stated before, the IRS says little about what assets are acceptable for an IRA, but they do state what is disallowed. Life insurance contracts and collectibles are not allowed. Knowing what is not allowed can help you when it comes to planning out your SDIRA.

The reason why some collectibles are accepted and some aren't comes down the purity of the investment. If we are talking about coins or precious metals, it is the purity that will dictate whether they can be brought into the SDIRA.

Life insurance contracts are not allowed to be IRA investments because they fundamentally contradict the purpose of an IRA, which is to provide financial security for retirement. The IRS regulations governing IRAs are designed to ensure that the funds within these accounts are used to accumulate savings that will support the account holder during their retirement years.

Life insurance, on the other hand, is primarily intended to provide a financial benefit to beneficiaries upon the death of the insured rather than to serve as a retirement savings vehicle for the policyholder. Allowing life insurance contracts as IRA investments would complicate the tax-deferred growth benefits of IRAs, introduce elements of risk not aligned with retirement savings goals, and potentially allow for premature withdrawals or misuse of funds. Therefore, the IRS excludes life insurance from being held in IRAs to maintain the integrity and intended use of these accounts for long-term retirement savings.

If you are a real estate investor and want to use your IRA to invest in a property, it may be a good idea, but you must be careful. Keep your eye out for red flags.

Here is a good example. Say a son's IRA is the buyer of the real estate. The broker of record is his father. The problem in this scenario is that his father is classified as a disallowed person. The IRA cannot do business with the father. Plus, if the father wants a commission for being the broker of record, that would also be benefitting a disallowed person.

Because this would be a prohibited transaction, we just couldn't allow that transaction to go through. This is an example of a common mistake account holders can make. They forget that normal investing rules do not always apply to IRA investing. This is also where having a competent self-directed retirement advisor becomes important. Before you get into a transaction using your self-directed account, discuss this with your administrator first.

Too many people think that when they implement an SDIRA, they no longer need to be involved. A self-directed account is not passive. You should always be prepared to be involved, even when you have financial advisors working for you. "Self-directed" means involvement. The responsibility for doing due diligence regarding investments and using one's SDIRA rests on the account holder's shoulders. Period.

WHAT YOU (THE INVESTOR) DO:

- Completes all the homework on the investment risk
- Chooses the investment
- Conducts all due diligence
- Negotiates the price of the asset
- Makes sure investments are not prohibited by IRS
- Makes all investments in the name of the IRA account
- Makes sure transactions don't include disqualified persons
- Monitors the account
- Completes documents or has them completed

SERVICES A CUSTODIAN/ADMINISTRATOR PROVIDES:

- Administers the sales and purchases of assets and processes invoices
- Administers account contributions and distributions
- Provides accurate and timely IRS reporting
- Provides IRA account recordkeeping
- Provides an online statement available 24/7

WHAT A CUSTODIAN/ADMINISTRATOR DOES NOT DO:

- Endorse any particular product or company
- Offer products or recommend investments
- Provide tax or investment advice
- Provide legal or financial advice
- Supply investment templates
- Complete or alter account holder's forms or legal documents

Let me take a step back and share with you an example of another prohibited transaction involving SDIRAs. This is a prime example of the indirect rule, that is, trying to do a transaction indirectly that you cannot do directly.

A potential account holder came to me wanting to take their 401(k) from their previous employer and roll it over into an SDIRA for the purpose of loaning money.

"Great," I said. "Who would you like to lend the money to?"

The man replied, "My sister-in-law."

"A sister-in-law is an allowed person. She is outside the family tree, so that's okay."

At that point, something told me to dig a little deeper. "Tell me, what will your sister-in-law do with the money when she gets it?"

I am so glad I inquired. His response made it a no-go. He said, "She's going to invest it in my company."

That is a prohibited transaction, and we couldn't move forward.

The deal violates the IRS indirect rule. If you can't do the deal directly, you can't do it indirectly either. This man would have received personal benefits from his IRA, and that makes the whole thing a prohibited transaction.

An individual retirement account is for the sole purpose of retirement, so benefiting from an IRA before retirement is frowned upon by the governing bodies.

Additionally, you cannot offer goods, services, or facilities to the plan. That's how it's written in Internal Revenue Code 4975.

For example, say your IRA is buying real estate. If you want to be the broker of record, even if for free, you are offering "services to the plan." That is disallowed because you are personally benefiting from the asset of your own retirement account.

Alternatively, say you use your IRA to buy a house and you wish to complete a remodel yourself. You might think that saving money and doing the work yourself is the way to go, but it's not. That's called an overcontribution of sweat equity. It's a big no-no! You cannot provide services to the plan, whether those services are paid for or you provide them at no cost.

Now let's say your IRA has invested in a vacation home, and you want to finally retire and reside there. Your IRA owns the property outright. Can you just move in and live there? Yes, but you need to do a few things first. You can't just buy the property from your IRA, because that's a prohibited transaction. You have to get an appraisal for the value of that property first, then you would withdraw the house at the market value. Later, your custodian will send a tax form called a 1099, which describes the value of the property, and only then could you own it personally. The 1099 form ensures that the IRS is aware of the transaction because this transaction is taxable to you as a distribution of IRA assets.

When obtaining a piece of real estate or other assets personally from your IRA, this is the preferred and acceptable way of making sure a person stays in compliance with the IRS rules. If people don't follow the rules, then they no longer have an IRA.

If the IRS deems a prohibited transaction has been committed, the IRA will cease to exist. If this happens, all of the funds are now taxable, and the former account holder will be issued a 1099 for them. It is far better to follow the rules and always do the due diligence necessary when using an IRA in an investment.

Let's talk about due diligence for a moment. When opening an SDIRA, you need to do your research on the custodian (or the administrator). Google the person and company. Do a search using the keyword "fraud" after their name. You might think this is a no-brainer, but my team and I have heard stories that would curl your hair.

Once you've selected a responsible administrator for your IRA, the next thing to do is look at the numbers—the hard numbers. You have to make sure everything jives. What does that mean? Let's say that you're investing in a particular asset. What are the acquisition costs? Is there adequate cash in the IRA to take care of expenses that the asset may incur? All expenses of the IRA need to be paid for by the IRA.

For a comprehensive understanding of the acquisition costs associated with investing in a particular asset using an IRA, it's important to consider all the potential expenses that may arise during the purchase and ownership phases. Here's a detailed list of common acquisition and ongoing costs to consider.

Acquisition Costs

- Purchase price: The actual cost of buying the asset
- Real estate broker fees: Commissions paid to brokers or agents for facilitating the transaction
- Closing costs: Fees associated with the finalization of a real estate transaction, including title insurance, escrow fees, recording fees, and notary fees
- Inspection fees: Costs for professional inspections, such as home inspections, pest inspections, or structural assessments
- Appraisal fees: Charges for an appraisal to determine the fair market value of the property
- Legal fees: Fees paid to attorneys for preparing and reviewing contracts, conducting due diligence, or advising on the purchase
- Survey costs: Fees for land surveys to determine property boundaries or verify legal descriptions
- Title insurance: Protection against potential legal issues with the property title
- Transfer taxes: Taxes imposed by local or state governments for transferring property ownership
- Financing costs: If applicable, costs associated with obtaining a loan, such as origination fees, points, and other lender charges
- Environmental assessment fees: Costs for environmental studies to ensure there are no hazardous conditions on the property
- HOA fees: Initial fees or dues paid to homeowners associations when acquiring a property within a managed community

Ongoing Expenses

- Property management fees: Fees paid to a property manager or management company for overseeing the property
- Maintenance and repairs: Costs for regular upkeep, repairs, and maintenance of the asset
- Insurance costs: Ongoing premiums for property insurance, liability insurance, or other required coverage
- Property taxes: Annual taxes assessed by local municipalities on the property
- Utilities: Payments for water, electricity, gas, and other essential services if the property is not tenant occupied or the IRA is responsible for these expenses
- HOA fees: Regular dues for properties in communities governed by homeowners associations
- Professional services: Fees for accountants, legal advisors, or other professionals who assist with managing the asset
- Advertising and marketing costs: Expenses for promoting the property for rent or sale
- Leasing fees: Costs associated with finding and securing tenants, if applicable

Other Potential Costs

- Eviction costs: Legal and administrative costs if tenants need to be evicted
- Vacancy costs: Lost income and potential expenses while the property is unoccupied
- Renovation and improvement costs: Any capital expenditures needed to enhance the property's value or functionality

It's crucial to ensure that the IRA has sufficient liquidity to cover these expenses, as all costs related to the investment must be paid directly from the IRA. It is often recommended to keep 10 percent of the property value in the account as a wad of idle cash. This helps maintain compliance with IRS rules and protects the tax-advantaged status of the account.

It's one thing to do your due diligence on the front end on an asset, but it's also important to do your due diligence on the back end. We saw a case where people didn't do their due diligence on the back end on a piece of real estate, and it was never recorded. That means the IRA didn't have title to the asset.

After acquiring an asset, especially within an IRA, it's crucial to perform due diligence to ensure all aspects of the acquisition are correctly handled and documented. Here's a comprehensive list of due diligence steps to take after the acquisition of an asset.

Post-Acquisition Due Diligence Steps

1. CONFIRM PROPER TITLE RECORDING

- Verify that the asset's title is recorded in the name of the IRA, not in the personal name of the IRA holder or any disqualified person
- Ensure that the title reflects the custodian's name as trustee or custodian for the IRA, according to IRS rules

2. REVIEW CLOSING DOCUMENTS

- Carefully review all closing documents to ensure accuracy and completeness. This includes the deed, settlement statement, purchase agreement, and any transfer documents
- Ensure all parties have signed all necessary documents and that they are correctly notarized, if required

3. OBTAIN TITLE INSURANCE POLICY

- Ensure that the title insurance policy is issued in the name of the IRA. Title insurance protects against any future claims or disputes regarding ownership

4. UPDATE PROPERTY INSURANCE

- Verify that appropriate property insurance policies are in place and that the IRA is listed as the insured party
- Check that the insurance coverage is adequate and aligns with the requirements of the investment property or asset

5. TRANSFER UTILITIES AND SERVICES

- If applicable, ensure that all utilities (water, electricity, gas, etc.) are transferred to the IRA or property management company, depending on how the asset is managed

- Arrange for any necessary property maintenance services and ensure contracts are in the name of the IRA

6. UPDATE RECORDS AND ACCOUNTING

- Maintain accurate and up-to-date records of the acquisition, including financial transactions, property deeds, and any related documents
- Record all expenses paid by the IRA for the asset to ensure proper tracking and compliance with IRS rules

7. COMPLIANCE WITH LOCAL REGULATIONS

- Confirm that the asset complies with all local regulations, zoning laws, and homeowners association rules, if applicable
- Obtain any necessary permits or licenses required for the asset

8. REVIEW FINANCING AGREEMENTS

- If the acquisition involves financing, review the loan documents to ensure that they are in compliance with IRS rules, especially regarding nonrecourse loans
- Confirm the loan terms, payment schedules, and any requirements or covenants associated with the financing

9. ENGAGE PROFESSIONAL MANAGEMENT

- If not already done, hire a qualified property manager or management company to oversee the asset
- Ensure that the management agreement is signed by the IRA custodian on behalf of the IRA

10. SCHEDULE REGULAR ASSET REVIEWS

- Plan regular reviews of the asset's performance, condition, and compliance to ensure ongoing due diligence
- Monitor market conditions and the asset's value to make informed decisions about holding or selling the investment

11. CHECK FOR ANY OUTSTANDING LIABILITIES

- Confirm there are no outstanding liens, debts, or obligations attached to the asset that could impact the IRA's ownership or value

- Conduct a final search for any encumbrances that may have been missed during the acquisition process

12. COORDINATE WITH IRA CUSTODIAN

- Maintain communication with the IRA custodian to ensure all transactions, payments, and asset management activities are correctly handled in accordance with IRS regulations
- Update the custodian with any changes or requirements related to the asset

By following these due diligence steps after acquiring an asset, you can ensure that your IRA investment is properly managed, compliant with regulations, and positioned for optimal performance.

BOTTOM LINE:
Make sure you select the right custodian (or administrator) and follow the rules set by the IRS regarding IRAs, so you don't end up owing money you didn't intend to spend out of your nest egg.

The IRA Sixty-Day Rule

Navigating IRAs requires an understanding of specific rules designed to preserve the tax-advantaged status of these accounts. One such rule is the sixty-day rollover rule, which plays a crucial role when transferring funds between retirement accounts. In general, if you withdraw funds from an IRA, you have sixty days to redeposit the money into another eligible retirement account to avoid taxes and potential penalties. But what happens if you miss the deadline? The IRS does provide some flexibility through exceptions, particularly in cases of unforeseen circumstances, errors by financial institutions, or military service.

WHAT IS THE SIXTY-DAY RULE FOR IRAS?

The sixty-day rule applies to rollovers from one IRA to another or between other eligible retirement accounts. Essentially, if you withdraw funds from an IRA with the intent to roll them over into another retirement account, you must complete the rollover within sixty days to avoid the amount being treated as a taxable distribution.

For example, if you take a distribution from your IRA on July 1, you must deposit the entire amount into another IRA or qualified retirement account by August 30. If the rollover is not completed within that sixty-day window, the withdrawn funds are subject to ordinary income taxes, and if you're under the age of 59½, you could also face a 10 percent early withdrawal penalty.

The good news is that, under certain conditions, the IRS offers relief through a few key exceptions to the sixty-day rule.

KEY EXCEPTIONS TO THE IRA SIXTY-DAY RULE:

- IRS waiver for unforeseen circumstances: The IRS provides waivers for taxpayers who miss the sixty-day rollover deadline due to unforeseen or uncontrollable circumstances. These circumstances can include severe illness, natural disasters, death, or other significant life events that prevent you from completing the rollover in time. In these situations, you can apply for a waiver from the IRS, explaining why you missed the deadline. If the IRS grants the waiver, they will provide additional time for you to complete the rollover without facing taxes or penalties.

- Financial institution errors: Errors made by financial institutions are another common reason the IRS grants relief from the sixty-day rule. For example, if the bank or brokerage responsible for processing your rollover makes an administrative error—such as failing to complete the transfer on time—the IRS may extend the sixty-day window. To qualify for this exception, you need to demonstrate that the failure was due to an error by the financial institution and that you followed up on the rollover in a timely manner. The IRS allows this relief to ensure taxpayers aren't penalized for mistakes outside of their control.

- Military service in combat zones: For military personnel deployed in a combat zone, the IRS offers a special extension to the sixty-day rollover period. This extension provides an additional 180 days after you leave the combat zone to complete the rollover. This exception acknowledges the unique challenges faced by military personnel in active duty, giving them more time to manage their finances without risking tax penalties.

- Automatic rollover from plan termination: When an employer terminates a retirement plan, such as a 401(k), they may automatically roll over the funds into an IRA. In these cases, the sixty-day rollover rule does not apply, as the funds are automatically moved without any action required from the account holder. This automatic rollover provides a seamless transition of retirement funds without concern for missed deadlines.
- Direct rollover between retirement accounts: A direct rollover is another strategy that can help you avoid the sixty-day rule altogether. This is when your retirement funds are transferred directly from one retirement account to another without you taking possession of the funds. Since you never touch the money, there is no risk of missing the sixty-day window, and the transaction is not subject to taxes or penalties. Direct rollovers are typically the safest and most efficient way to move funds between retirement accounts and are highly recommended to avoid the complications of indirect rollovers.

THE IMPORTANCE OF TIMING AND PROACTIVE MANAGEMENT

Understanding the sixty-day rule and the exceptions available is essential for effective retirement account management. Missing the sixty-day deadline can result in your withdrawal being classified as a taxable event, which could lead to significant taxes and penalties, particularly if you're under the age of 59½.

Being proactive and mindful of the timeline for rollovers can save you from these financial setbacks. If unforeseen circumstances arise, it's crucial to act quickly and consult with a financial advisor to explore your options, including whether you qualify for an exception.

REQUESTING A WAIVER: WHAT YOU NEED TO KNOW

If you believe you qualify for a waiver of the sixty-day rule due to unforeseen circumstances, you'll need to file a private letter ruling (PLR) with the IRS. This involves a formal application explaining the reason for the missed deadline and providing supporting documentation. The IRS will review your case and determine whether to grant the waiver.

Keep in mind that filing for a PLR can be a complex process, and it's advisable to work with a tax professional to ensure your application is properly prepared.

Safeguarding Your Retirement Funds

The IRA sixty-day rollover rule is designed to protect the tax-deferred status of retirement accounts, but it can present challenges for those managing multiple accounts or facing unforeseen life events. Fortunately, the IRS provides several exceptions to this rule, offering relief in cases of financial institution errors, military service, and more.[43]

To avoid potential tax liabilities, always stay aware of the sixty-day timeline when moving funds between retirement accounts. When in doubt, opt for a direct rollover or consult with a financial advisor to explore your options. Taking a proactive approach to retirement planning will help ensure that your savings continue to grow and support your financial future.

---

[43] "Tax Exempt Bonds Private Letter Rulings: Some Basic Concepts," Internal Revenue Service, accessed September 16, 2024, https://www.irs.gov/tax-exempt-bonds/teb-private-letter-ruling-some-basic-concepts#:~:text=A%20private%20letter%20ruling%2C%20or,taxpayers%20or%20by%20IRS%20personnel.

Chapter 8

UDFI Tax and Leveraging Your IRA

*"People without leverage work for those with leverage.
The same can be said about money."*

Should You Leverage Your IRA Money?

Though the IRS has strict rules on how much each person can contribute toward retirement accounts each year, there are things that can be done to leverage your retirement money to further accelerate its investing power.

Most real estate investors and real estate professionals are certainly familiar with the concept of leverage. However, the average investor is not.

As mentioned in Chapter 6, "leverage" is the use of borrowed capital to increase the potential return of an investment. In the real estate world, that means using part equity and part retirement money to purchase an investment property. Wouldn't it be great if we could legally use our IRA money as a down payment and then leverage to buy a rental property? There are ways to leverage the funds in an IRA to do just that.

Leveraging Your IRA

What if you have a healthy amount of money that has accumulated within your IRA over the years, but it is not enough to purchase the rental property that you want to purchase? Do you need to wait several more years to accumulate the rest of the money before they buy that rental property? The answer is no. Currently, it is possible for you to use your IRA funds as well as borrowed money to purchase the rental property. This is called "leveraging your IRA."

Let's use the example of one investor we'll call James. Over the years, James has accumulated roughly $250,000 in his work 401(k). At the age of 60, he decides to do an in-service rollover and move his money from his employer-based 401(k) into an SDIRA. James knows he could buy a small rental in his local area for $200,000. However, he feels that there might be significant appreciation in the next few years in this particular market. Instead of using all of his IRA money to purchase one rental property, James wants to leverage his IRA and instead purchase two rentals for $200,000 each. Since he does not have $400,000 in his IRA, he decides to use his IRA to obtain nonrecourse loans. Once the loans are approved, James's IRA is the proud owner of two single-family rentals in a nearby town!

Not only is James's $200,000 of IRA funds growing for him tax deferred, the IRA also has $200,000 of borrowed money that is also growing for him on a tax-deferred basis. This strategy can be a great loophole if implemented correctly. Conversely, if implemented incorrectly, this strategy may end up costing James quite a bit of money.

So how is it possible that James's IRA can end up costing him in taxes? Great question. What many investors are surprised to find out is that IRAs can also be subject to taxes. In fact, an IRA may be subject to taxes even when no distributions are taken out of the retirement account.

In James's example, the two rentals could generate, say, a net taxable profit of $20,000 for the year after all expenses. The IRA will need to pay the IRS a tax known as an unrelated debt-financed income tax (a.k.a. UDFI taxes). This is because some of the income is a result of using leverage to produce some of the net taxable profit. There is no tax paid on the net taxable profit earned by the IRA money, only on the profit earned by using leverage.

What Is Unrelated Debt-Financed Income Tax?

Unrelated debt-financed income tax (UDFI) is a tax imposed on income generated in association with debt in a retirement account. This can include rental income as well as capital gains from the sale of a rental property. It is important to note that UDFI is not only associated with acquisition debt upon the purchase of a property. UDFI can also be imposed on refinance debt as well as construction or improvement debt. For example, if James had purchased one rental with all cash and the IRA did a cash-out refinance to pull out some cash from the rental, then that rental property might now be subject to UDFI taxes.

Debt is debt regardless of who the lender is. Whether James's IRA is borrowing from a big bank or from his sister, he may want to speak with his tax advisor to determine any UDFI tax exposures.

So why does this tax exist? Simply to make sure that non-retirement money does not escape the normal income taxation laws of the U.S.

government each year. As you can see in the above example, the profit that is attributable to the IRA's equity ownership is still tax deferred. However, the profit attributable to the IRA's leveraged ownership is technically not IRA money and is thus subject to IRS taxes each year.

Calculating UDFI Taxes

If you want to understand how UDFI taxes are calculated and how much an account holder can expect to pay, here are some high-level steps for the calculation:

1. Determine the taxable income for the property for the year. Please note this is the net taxable income—for example, rental income received minus mortgage interest, property taxes, repair costs, management fees, depreciation, and other common rental property expenses.

$$\text{Taxable Income} = \text{Rental income} - \begin{array}{l} \text{(Mortgage Interest + Property Taxes +} \\ \text{Repair Costs + Management Fees +} \\ \text{Depreciation + and Other Expenses)} \end{array}$$

Definitions:

- **Rental income**: The total income received from renting out the property
- **Mortgage interest**: The interest portion of the mortgage payments for the year
- **Property taxes**: The total property taxes paid for the year
- **Repair costs**: The total cost of repairs made to the property during the year
- **Management fees**: Fees paid for property management services
- **Depreciation**: The allowable depreciation expense for the property for the year
- **Other expenses**: Any additional common rental property expenses such as insurance, utilities paid by the owner, etc.

This equation subtracts all the allowable expenses from the rental income to calculate the net taxable income for the property.

2. Determine the average debt balance for the year. Add up the amount of debt outstanding on the first day of each month during the year that the retirement account owned the property. Then divide that total by the total number of months during the tax year that the retirement account owned the property.

$$\text{Average Debt Balance} = \frac{\text{Sum of Debt Balances at the Beginning of Each Month}}{\text{Total Number of Months}}$$

3. Determine the average adjusted tax basis of the property. The adjusted tax basis of the property represents the total cost of the property, plus improvements, minus any depreciation taken cumulatively. The average adjusted basis is the average of the adjusted basis of the property on the first and last days during the tax year that the retirement account owned the property.

$$\text{Average Adjusted Basis} = \frac{\text{Adjusted Basis on the Day 1} + \text{Adjusted Basis on the Day 365}}{2}$$

4. Determine the debt ratio. To calculate this amount, divide the average debt amount (step 2) by the average adjusted basis of the property (step 3).

$$\text{Debt Ratio} = \frac{\text{Average Debt Balance}}{\text{Average Adjusted Basis}}$$

5. Once steps 1 through 4 are complete, these amounts are used to calculate the ratio of the net taxable income that is subject to UDFI taxes. Multiple the debt ratio (step 4) times the taxable income (step 1). This is the amount of the net taxable income that is subject to UDFI taxes.

Once the leveraged portion of the net taxable income subject to UDFI taxes has been calculated (step 5), what's next? How much should your retirement account expect to pay Uncle Sam for UDFI taxes?

The first $1,000 of the step 5 amount is tax free (i.e., each retirement account does not have to pay UDFI taxes on the first $1,000 of its net taxable income each year). Then if the remaining leveraged portion of taxable income subject to UDFI taxes is between $0 and $12,950, your retirement account should expect to pay a tax rate of 10–35 percent to the IRS. For any amount of taxable income in excess of $12,950, your retirement account should expect to pay a tax rate of 37 percent to the IRS on such an amount.

How will this impact James? Let's look at a few scenarios.

Scenario 1: Taxable profit—Assume that the leveraged portion of James's IRA's net taxable profit for the year from its two rental properties was $10,000 (step 5). The first $1,000 is tax free. So on the remaining $9,000, he should probably expect to pay $1,540 in UDFI taxes to Uncle Sam for that tax year.

Scenario 2: No taxable profit—Assume instead that the leveraged portion of James's IRA's net taxable profit for the year was $0 instead of $9,000. (Maybe the IRA was able to increase the depreciation deductions on the two rental properties.) The IRA shouldn't have to pay any UDFI taxes for that year.

Scenario 3: Loss instead of profit—Assume that the leveraged portion of James's IRA's net taxable profit for the year from its two rental properties was negative, meaning there was a net taxable loss of $3,000 instead of a profit. This could happen if the expenses, including depreciation, mortgage interest, property taxes, repair costs, management fees, and other deductible expenses exceeded the rental income generated by the properties.

Since the net taxable profit is $0 or less, the IRA would not be subject to UDFI taxes for that year. Additionally, the $3,000 loss could potentially be carried forward to offset future taxable income, depending on the tax rules and regulations that apply to IRAs. Thus, James's IRA wouldn't have to pay any UDFI taxes for that year.

To Leverage or Not to Leverage . . .

Should you avoid using leverage in retirement accounts?

Not necessarily. Deciding whether to use leverage for an investment property within an IRA is a significant decision that should be made in consultation with your tax advisors after careful analysis. This decision can be influenced by several factors, including the amount of available funds, the expected return on one property compared to another, and the anticipated expenses associated with a particular property.

Thanks to the ability to deduct rental-related expenses and claim depreciation, many retirement accounts that use leverage end up paying little to no UDFI taxes in the end. It's important to remember that the earnings within your IRA are growing on a tax-deferred basis; only the income generated through the use of leverage may be subject to taxation.

Now let's look at the right and wrong ways to use leverage in retirement accounts.

Get the Right Type of Loan

As indicated previously, the retirement account is a distinct entity from the account holder. As such, when SDIRA money is used to purchase a rental property, the title of the property would be held by the IRA and not the individual account holder. It is no different when it comes to loans for retirement account–owned real estate. Just like when purchasing real estate, the loan must be made to the IRA and not the IRA owner.

The hard-and-fast rule is that the account holder cannot be involved in the transaction at all when it comes to IRA-owned real estate. The account holder:

- Cannot be on title to the property.
- Cannot be a signer on the loan.
- Cannot personally guarantee the loan.
- Cannot provide personal assets as collateral for the retirement loan.

The loan obtained by the IRA must be a nonrecourse loan. This means that the bank cannot go after the account holder in any way if the IRA defaults on the loan. The only recourse on the bank's side is to foreclose on the property itself.

It is extremely important to understand this rule. Otherwise, the account holder would be construed as having committed a prohibited transaction. This could subject the owner's entire retirement account funds to distribution taxes and potential penalties.

Always remember that the IRA is viewed legally as completely separate from the IRA account holder. As such, all funds due with respect to the purchase and leverage of this property, such as down payment, earnest money, closing costs, loan fees, inspection fees, and appraisal fees, as well as any UDFI taxes, need to come from the IRA directly.

Reduce the Loan Amount

If an IRA-owned rental starts to generate positive taxable income after its expenses, the account holder should consider paying off or reducing the loan within the IRA. Since UDFI taxes are calculated based on the average debt balance for any given year, lowering the loan balance by December 31 can significantly reduce UDFI taxes. By paying down the debt, the leveraged portion of the income is reduced, which in turn lowers the amount of income subject to UDFI taxes.

In fact, if the account holder owns a rental in the IRA that they plan to sell at a significant gain, paying off the loan and waiting to sell a year later can potentially eliminate any UDFI tax liabilities, as the absence of debt removes the leverage that triggers UDFI taxation.

Roth IRAs Do Not Escape the Tax

Many investors mistakenly believe that because Roth IRAs are tax-free accounts that this means Roth IRAs are also exempt from UDFI taxes. It is important to note that this is an incorrect assumption. Although a Roth IRA is permanently free from income taxes, it is still subject to UDFI taxes when leverage is used within the IRA, as the net taxable income earned from leverage is taxable.

IRAs May Still Be Subject to Income Taxes Upon Distribution

On a similar note, some people believe that if their IRA pays UDFI taxes, then the future distributions from that retirement account would not be subject to income taxes. This, again, is an incorrect assumption, because future distributions from a traditional IRA are generally still subject to income taxes.

An easy way to remember this is to understand that income taxes and UDFI taxes are two completely different taxes. Income taxes are assessed on distributions when funds are withdrawn from the IRA, while UDFI taxes are levied on the income generated from leveraging within the IRA itself.

Don't Forget the State

In addition to the IRS wanting its share of UDFI taxes from leveraged retirement account profits, some states may also require retirement accounts to pay their own state-related UDFI taxes. This would usually be applicable to the state in which the rental property is located. It is always best to consult with a tax advisor on these matters.

Using Solo 401(k) to Avoid Paying UDFI Taxes

Did you know there is an easy way to use leverage in retirement accounts and avoid UDFI taxes altogether? It is simply to invest with a solo 401(k) instead of an IRA.

Remember that a solo 401(k) is a retirement plan for self-employed people who don't have any employees other than a spouse. It's a popular option for independent entrepreneurs because it offers substantial tax benefits and contribution limits.

This is one of the loopholes within the IRS code that indicates qualified plans, such as 401(k)s, are allowed to invest using leverage while escaping UDFI taxes of up to 37 percent.

If the account holder is eligible for a solo-k, they should consider moving their funds from their IRA to their solo-k prior to investing in leveraged real estate to minimize or potentially eliminate UDFI taxes.

This is where being knowledgeable about all the rules comes in handy. There are some very powerful ways that retirement money can be used for real estate investing. Not only can the account holder have full control of their retirement funds, but they can also leverage the velocity of their retirement money to supercharge the return using debt and other financing techniques! In my world, that's exciting stuff.

> **NOTE:**
> *To avoid any unpleasant tax surprises, be sure to strategize with your attorney or tax advisor before pulling the trigger on any advanced investing techniques.*

Chapter 9

Real Estate Investment and Retirement Planning

"Real estate offers a unique blend of security and growth potential, making it a powerful tool for retirement planning. By investing wisely, you're not just buying property—you're building your future wealth."

—Scott Trench, author of *Set for Life*

If you're self-directing, be prepared to be involved. Unlike traditional retirement accounts where investments are managed by financial professionals, a self-directed IRA or 401(k) requires you to take an active role in your investment decisions. This means you'll need to research potential investments thoroughly, understand the rules and regulations governing self-directed accounts, and monitor your portfolio regularly. It's crucial to stay informed and engaged to maximize your returns and avoid any compliance pitfalls. Being actively involved also means being ready to make decisions quickly and strategically to seize opportunities and address challenges as they arise.

In this chapter, I will address the following common questions when it comes to real estate and retirement planning.

- What is real estate's place in a good retirement plan?
- What are the benefits of real estate investing for retirement?
- What goals and strategies can help keep individuals on track?
- How are the gains and proceeds accessed through a self-directed retirement account?
- How easy is it for heirs to access these funds and assets when it comes time to receive their inheritance?

The Role of Real Estate in Retirement Planning

Real estate plays a substantial role in everyone's retirement plan. We all need somewhere to live. Most Americans' net worth winds up being in their residences. Harvard and MIT professor Robert C. Merton and other leading economic minds have more recently begun to pose that a home could be a source of alternative pension funding.[44] If homes are owned free and clear at retirement, they may be tapped into for income using reverse mortgages.

However, more and more Americans are retiring with free and clear homes. Statistics show that as of 2022, 38.5 percent of owner-occupied homes did not have a mortgage.[45] This means that only 38.5 percent of homeowners were living mortgage free—and carrying significantly less debt than those with a mortgage—during the five-year period of data that was collected.

However, according to AARP, using Federal Reserve data, Americans across generations are carrying more debt overall than they did three decades ago, but the rise has been especially steep among the oldest age groups.[46]

This all creates even more pressure on individuals and couples to demand more from their investments. It also points to the need of real estate as a pure investment vehicle inside a retirement portfolio (in addition to owning a home).

Real estate investments help provide portfolio diversification, as well as the potential for generating both passive income and capital gains in retirement.

The Benefits of Real Estate Investing for Retirement

There are varieties of drivers that attract individuals to real estate investments, especially when it comes to preparing for retirement and beyond.

- **Passive income.** The most significant and urgent need for retirees is passive income. It is also crucial to remember that projected retirement dates often don't match up with reality. It is vital to be prepared early. The passive income potential of real estate can ensure that it is in place well in advance of retirement, even without having the largest nest egg.

[44] Robert C. Merton and Arun Muralidhar, "SeLFIES: A New Pension Bond and Currency for Retirement," Harvard Law School Forum on Corporate Governance, May 20, 2020, https://corpgov.law.harvard.edu/2020/05/20/selfies-a-new-pension-bond-and-currency-for-retirement/.

[45] U.S. Census Bureau, "Mortgage Status," *American Community Survey, ACS 5-Year Estimates Detailed Tables, Table B25081, 2022*, https://data.census.gov/table/ACSDT5Y2022.B25081.

[46] U.S. Census Bureau, "Mortgage Status."

- **Wealth building.** While most experts would advise against making speculative investments based on possible future valuations, real estate is regarded as one of the best investment vehicles for keeping up with inflation. Though real estate values constantly fluctuate, long-term graphs show that values have consistently risen over time. Data also shows that rents (while volatile) trend upward. Increasing yields and cash flow spreads alone increase value from an investment perspective.

Median Sales Price of Houses Sold for the United States

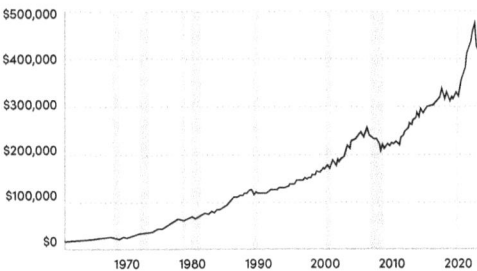

Image source: "Median Sales Price of Houses Sold for the United States," FRED: Federal Reserve Bank of St. Louis, updated July 24, 2024, https://fred.stlouisfed.org/series/MSPUS.

National Single-Family Rent Index Year-Over-Year Percent Change By Price Tier

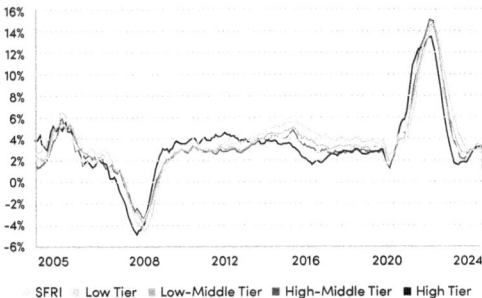

SFRI Low Tier Low-Middle Tier High-Middle Tier High Tier

Image source: "Single-Family Rent Growth Tripled Year Over Year in December, CoreLogic Reports," CoreLogic, February 15, 2022, https://www.corelogic.com/press-releases/single-family-rent-growth-tripled-year-over-year-in-december-corelogic-reports/.

- **Low volatility.** While real estate can provide sprints in capital gains over a period of years and may slip in value in other years, this volatility is far more gradual and predictable than many other types of investments.
- **Diversification.** Real estate provides critical diversification from stocks, bonds, gold, and even cash. When stock values are crushed, real estate often goes up. If cash is devalued, real estate prices can go up. Having real estate in a portfolio ensures stability and hedges against losses in other sectors.
- **Safety.** What really differentiates real estate from many other investment vehicles is its safety level. While it is true that hurricanes, fires, terror attacks, and earthquakes can destroy buildings, even then insurance often covers a great deal of that damage, and the land is rarely impacted. The land is often where the majority of the value is. This brick-and-mortar and terra firma security means it is essentially always there. There is always a tangible asset. Stocks can completely evaporate, cash can be stolen or burned up, and businesses can go bankrupt. Yet, regardless of its current value, real estate is still there. Some types of real estate investment even enjoy better protection from legal issues such as bankruptcy and judgments.
- **Leverage.** One of my favorites, leverage can be used in stocks but is most notable in real estate. Real estate financing via partnerships, mortgages, business loans, and lines of credit are all used to leverage control of more property assets and income. There are normally debt service and loan costs involved but being able to control larger assets—and to benefit from their cash flow—can enable investors to grow their portfolios more rapidly.
- **Taxes.** Real estate is popular for its tax breaks. It is important for individual investors to consult their own tax professionals and accountants to see which breaks still apply if they are also using a retirement account or other vehicles to invest. However, there are many potential real estate tax breaks. These include depreciation, management fees, interest, and more. You can learn more about the complexities and benefits of real estate tax strategies in *The Book on*

Tax Strategies for the Savvy Real Estate Investor by Amanda Han and Matthew MacFarland (www.BiggerPockets.com/ReadTaxSavvy).

- **Control over assets.** One of the unique features of this asset class is the level of control investors have over their assets. In real estate, this applies to both income and value. Most individual investors have no hope of ever being able to impact the value or performance of their stocks or gold. They may be able to influence their small businesses investments, but that can be far less predictable than in real estate. Via positioning and marketing, value-adding improvement, and superior management, owners can increase the profitability, cash flow, and resale value of their properties. This applies in every market and every market phase.

As you can see, there are many drivers and benefits derived from using one's IRA to invest in real estate. Now let's talk about a few things the account holder needs to know about reaching into their retirement funds.

Withdrawals

How do investors access the assets, gains, and yields from their real estate investments in their SDIRAs?

As with all retirement accounts, there is the ability to liquidate assets and make withdrawals at any time. However, there can be consequences. There are also required distributions, as well as special provisions for passing on retirement funds to beneficiaries. The more knowledgeable investors are about these factors, the better they can plan to achieve their goals.

Early Withdrawals

Investors may liquidate their retirement account holdings and withdraw funds as they choose. However, those under 59½ years of age will typically trigger an additional 10 percent tax on any early distribution amounts. Fortunately, there are multiple exceptions covering almost every urgent need. That means being able to earn returns on funds actively invested and growing, which would otherwise be collecting dust as cash. This can be a great selling feature for real estate professionals.

Exemptions from the 10 percent additional penalty are available for:

- **First-time homebuyers**. Up to $10,000 can be withdrawn for the purchase of and down payment on a home.
- **Education expenses**. Early withdrawals can be made to cover higher education expenses.
- **Health insurance**. Individuals who become unemployed for twelve weeks or more can make withdrawals to cover health insurance premiums for themselves and their immediate families.
- **Medical expenses**. Medical expenses not reimbursed by insurance coverage may be paid from an IRA if they exceed 7.5 percent of adjusted gross income.
- **Disability or death**. Funds may be withdrawn early penalty free if the account holder becomes disabled. Payments made to beneficiaries or the estate on death are not penalized.
- **Military reservists**. Military reservists may avoid penalties on early withdrawals if called to active duty for at least 180 days.
- **IRS levies**. If the IRS places a levy against the account holder and forces an involuntary withdrawal, they do not assess the penalty.
- **Periodic payments (aka the 72t)** . The account holder won't be penalized if they establish equal periodic payments/withdrawals for account owners and beneficiaries.

Similar exceptions are provided for Roth IRAs and 401(k)s, but to be on the safe side, check with your tax advisor and custodian in advance.

In addition to the existing penalty exceptions, the SECURE 2.0 Act, effective December 29, 2022, introduced new exceptions to the 10 percent early withdrawal penalty from retirement accounts. As a result, these changes increase flexibility for accessing funds, especially during hardships or emergencies.

Six New Exceptions Overview

1. **Public safety employees.** The age 50 penalty exception expands for these employees. It now includes private sector firefighters over 50, public safety workers under 50 with twenty-five years

of service, and state or local corrections officers and forensic personnel. From 2027, disabled first responders like law enforcement officers, firefighters, paramedics, and emergency medical personnel, can get gross income exclusions post retirement.

2. **Domestic abuse victims.** Starting in 2024, 401(k), 403(b), and governmental 457(b) plan participants who are domestic abuse victims can withdraw funds penalty free. The limit is $10,000 or 50 percent of the vested account balance, whichever is less, within a year of the abuse. Self-certification for eligibility is allowed.

3. **Terminally ill employees.** Distributions to terminally ill employees are penalty free. This applies if death is expected within eighty-four months, as certified by a physician.

4. **Federally declared disasters.** Withdrawals made within 180 days of a declared disaster are exempt from the 10 percent penalty. This applies if the participant's primary residence is in the disaster area and they have suffered an economic loss.

5. **Financial emergencies.** From 2024, up to $1,000 can be withdrawn annually from retirement plans for urgent financial needs. This is allowed if prior distributions are repaid or if subsequent contributions match the withdrawal amount. Another withdrawal is possible after three years if these conditions aren't met.

6. **Emergency savings accounts.** SECURE 2.0 allows emergency savings accounts in 401(k) and 403(b) plans for non–highly compensated participants. The maximum balance is $2,500, though sponsors may set lower limits.

Taking a Property Out of an IRA

One of the unique and lesser-known features of the SDIRA is being able to take a property out of the portfolio for personal use. The rules state that a property inside an IRA restricts personal use and cannot be used as a full-time personal residence. However, as outlined in Chapter 7, a property can be purchased earlier in life by the IRA, can be paid off from rental income, grow in value, and then may be taken out for use as a retirement home or for beneficiaries later on.

To complete this transfer, account holders need to:

- Obtain an appraisal from a qualified appraiser.
- Complete the withdrawal form, and provide the original, notarized document.
- Provide a deed for transferring the title to the property (i.e., a quit claim deed).

Required Minimum Distributions

The IRS has currently designed the system so that account holders are required to deplete their retirement accounts over their expected lifetimes. Required minimum distributions were made mandatory in 2003. These distribution amounts vary over time depending on average rate of return, life expectancy rates, and individual savings balances and ages. It is important to anticipate these changes as the government updates economic policy and monetary strategy.

This table lays out the minimum withdrawal schedules beginning at age 70½ as of 2024.

IRS Uniform Lifetime Table

Age	Life Expectancy Factor	Age	Life Expectancy Factor
70	27.4	93	9.8
71	26.5	94	9.1
72	25.6	95	8.6
73	24.7	96	8.1
74	23.8	97	7.6
75	22.9	98	7.1
76	22.0	99	6.7
77	21.2	100	6.3
78	26.3	101	5.9
79	19.5	102	5.5
80	18.7	103	5.2
81	17.9	104	4.9
82	17.1	105	4.5
83	16.3	106	4.2
84	15.5	107	3.9
85	14.8	108	3.7

Age	Life Expectancy Factor	Age	Life Expectancy Factor
86	14.1	109	3.4
87	13.4	110	3.1
88	12.7	111	2.9
89	12.0	112	2.6
90	11.4	113	2.4
91	10.8	114	2.1
92	10.2	115 & Older	1.9

Source: IRS Publication 590-B, Table III

$$\text{Your RMD} = \frac{\text{Account Balance (as of Dec 31 last year)}}{\text{Life Expectancy Factor (using the age you turn this year)}}$$

Image source: "Distributions from Individual Retirement Arrangements (IRAs)," Department of Treasury Internal Revenue Service, March 12, 2024, https://www.irs.gov/pub/irs-pdf/p590b.pdf.

NOTE:

There can be exceptions to these figures for 403(b) plan holders who are younger than 75 years old, and for those with a spouse who is the sole beneficiary of the account and who is ten or more years younger than the account holder.

Succession Planning

For many individuals, an IRA is a highly effective estate and succession-planning tool. These individuals may be more concerned with using SDIRAs to build wealth and passive income potential for heirs.

INHERITED IRAS

The most common way retirement account assets and funds are passed on to beneficiaries is through inheriting an IRA. An account holder can nominate multiple beneficiaries by percentages, as well as backup beneficiaries. These beneficiaries may be changed at any time.

Rules for inherited IRAs differ depending on whether the beneficiary is a spouse or not. As a surviving spouse, the individual may assume the IRA and make it his or her own, roll it over into a similar plan, or begin receiving distributions from the IRA. Distributions may also be rolled over to their own IRA (if completed within the sixty-day time limit).

If you inherit an IRA from someone other than a spouse, it cannot be assumed or transferred into your name. However, a trustee-to-trustee transfer may be possible in some cases to consolidate the estate and defer full liquidation. Additionally, for non-spouse beneficiaries, post-2007 rules may allow a rollover of an inherited 401(k) into an IRA. Another option could be to leave the inherited plan intact and take required minimum distributions, provided these begin within five years of the inheritance. Keep in mind that not all plan sponsors or administrators offer these options, so it's essential to verify the specifics with the plan administrator before you make any decisions.

Charitable Giving Through Your IRA

IRA account holders aged 70½ or older can make tax-free charitable donations directly from their IRAs through qualified charitable distributions (QCDs). By using a QCD, these account holders can donate up to $100,000 per year to eligible charities without the distribution being included in their taxable income. This provision allows them to support charitable causes without increasing their taxable income, offering a strategic way to fulfill their required minimum distributions (RMDs) while benefiting charities. Note that this option does not apply to donations that provide benefits to the donor, such as tickets to events or goods in return.

Real estate investment can be a powerful tool for retirement planning, offering unique opportunities to generate passive income, build wealth, and diversify a retirement portfolio. However, it also requires a hands-on approach, especially when utilizing SDIRAs or 401(k)s. Go through the complexities of investing in property within retirement accounts carefully, including understanding the benefits, risks, and tax implications of such investments. By staying informed and actively managing these assets, investors can optimize their retirement savings and create a more secure financial future. As we've explored in this chapter, the right strategies and careful planning can turn real estate into a cornerstone of a robust retirement plan, allowing you to enjoy the advantages of property ownership while ensuring their long-term financial stability.

Chapter 10

Tax-Saving Alternatives

"With great power comes great responsibility."

— Spider-Man

IRAs are a part of a suite of powerful and legal tools that the government and IRS expects individuals to use to protect themselves and their families from unfair tax burdens. It is thanks to tools like these that investors no longer need to drive themselves crazy with expensive and/or risky tax schemes or chains of questionable offshore shelter companies.

One benefit comes from globalization that is making the world smaller. As a result, old tax havens have been rendered unfriendly, which in turn has dramatically increased transparency. In fact, some major news outlets argue that the United States has become one of the top tax havens on the planet, as further evidenced by new anti-money-laundering and tax-evasion regulations meant to target private and corporate cash buyers.[47] In addition to SDIRAs, the following tools can provide protection from taxes in a safe, legal, simple, and affordable way.

1031 Exchanges

Named for section 1031 of the Internal Revenue Code (IRC), 1031 exchanges enable real estate investors to roll over capital gains into new properties and defer taxes. This can be an incredibly powerful tool for compounding gains over the long term with the freedom to exit and acquire properties at the optimum moments. As with an SDIRA, a 1031 exchange requires a third-party exchange service to act as an intermediary. There are also strict timelines that must be adhered to in order to preserve tax protections. In contrast to the SDIRA, the cons can include the need for advanced planning, having a limited number of properties that can be rolled into, and a lack of freedom to jump between different types of investments.

---

[47] "U.S. Regulators Tackle Money Laundering in the Luxury Home Market," *Thomson Reuters*, accessed September 16, 2024, https://legal.thomsonreuters.com/en/insights/articles/u-s-regulators-tackle-money-laundering-luxury-home-market.

LLCs

A limited liability company (LLC) is a business structure that offers limited liability protection and pass-through taxation. Like other legal entities, LLCs can qualify investors and small business owners for another level of tax deductions and write-offs including but not limited to the costs related to office space, travel and entertainment, business vehicles, wages paid to employees and contract workers, and marketing expenses. Read more in Chapter 17.

Reinsurance

Reinsurance is insurance purchased by insurance companies to mitigate their own risk. A captive is a wholly owned subsidiary established to provide insurance specifically for its parent company, functioning as a form of self-insurance where the insured owns the insurer. Reinsurance and captives have been utilized as advanced tax shelter tools for years. However, they appear to be winding down as lawmakers change rules around their use. New rules implemented in 2015 set new standards to qualify for tax breaks. In January 2016, one of New York's wealthiest billionaire hedge fund managers closed his Bermuda reinsurance firm. It may be better to skip this option for now.[48]

Trusts

A trust is an estate-planning tool that allows an individual to manage and protect assets for the benefit of heirs or other beneficiaries. Trusts can be a useful estate-planning tool for several reasons. A trust may provide efficient provision for heirs who may not be trusted to handle finances well. Trusts can streamline inheritances and shield assets. However, they may not be the tax-saving vehicle some believe them to be. Back in 2013, *Forbes* began warning individuals that new taxes were set to take an extra 8.8 percent bite out of gains and highlighted an exodus from these vehicles to avoid that.[49] This editorial enlightenment attempted to steer people clear of trusts when there is no evidence against the use of trusts. They are, in fact, a good tool. There

---

[48] Sonali Basak and Zachary R. Mider, "Paulson Reinsurer Winds Down After Slump, Tax Criticism," Bloomberg, January 13, 2016, http://www.bloomberg.com/news/articles/2016-01-13/paulson-reinsurer-winds-down-after-slump-bermuda-tax-criticism.

[49] Ashley Ebeling, "Tax Hikes Hit Trusts Hard, Beneficiaries Pull Money Out," *Forbes*, January 9, 2013, http://www.forbes.com/sites/ashleaebeling/2013/01/09/tax-hikes-hit-trusts-hard-beneficiaries-pull-money-out/#67471a4b2607.

are numerous trust structures to explore, especially for personal residences, even while media companies such as *Kiplinger* argue that the tax savings may not be what some expect.[50]

Here are a few relevant trust structures that real estate investors might consider using to optimize tax efficiency, protect assets, and plan for succession. Find a competent attorney to advise you and assist in with determining which trust structure is best.

Revocable Living Trust

🎯 PURPOSE

A revocable living trust allows the investor to retain control over their real estate assets during their lifetime while providing a clear mechanism for transferring those assets upon death without going through probate.

👥 ADVANTAGES

- Flexibility: The trust can be modified or revoked at any time.
- Probate avoidance: Assets in the trust bypass probate, providing a faster and private transfer to heirs.

💭 CONSIDERATIONS

While it avoids probate, a revocable trust does not offer asset protection from creditors during the grantor's lifetime.

Irrevocable Trust

🎯 PURPOSE

An irrevocable trust transfers ownership of the property to the trust, with the trust managed by a trustee, which can offer asset protection and tax benefits.

👥 ADVANTAGES

- Asset protection: Property placed in an irrevocable trust is typically shielded from creditors.
- Tax benefits: If properly structured, it may help reduce estate taxes and capital gains taxes.

---

[50] "Four Facts of Living Trusts," *Kiplinger Personal Finance*, December 31, 2014, http://www. kiplinger.com/article/retirement/T021-C000-S001-four-facts-of-living-trusts.html.

CONSIDERATIONS

Once assets are placed in an irrevocable trust, the terms generally cannot be changed, and control over the assets is given to the trustee.

Land Trust

PURPOSE

A land trust holds the title to real estate while keeping the owner's identity confidential. It's commonly used for real estate investment properties.

ADVANTAGES

- Privacy: The land trust keeps the real estate owner's name off public records.
- Ease of transfer: Beneficial interests in the trust can be transferred without recording a public change in ownership.

CONSIDERATIONS

While a land trust provides privacy, it does not inherently offer asset protection unless paired with other structures like LLCs.

Qualified Personal Residence Trust (QPRT)

PURPOSE

A QPRT allows the investor to transfer ownership of a primary residence or vacation home to the trust while continuing to live in the property for a specified period.

ADVANTAGES

- Estate tax reduction: The property is removed from the estate, reducing potential estate tax liability.
- Continued use: The grantor can continue living in the property rent free for a predetermined number of years.

CONSIDERATIONS

If the grantor outlives the term of the trust, they must pay rent to continue living in the home, but this also helps further reduce estate taxes.

Delaware Statutory Trust (DST)

🎯 PURPOSE

A DST is commonly used in real estate for fractional ownership of larger properties and can be utilized in 1031 exchange transactions.

👥 ADVANTAGES

- 1031 exchange eligible: DSTs are recognized for like-kind exchanges, making them a tool for deferring capital gains taxes.
- Passive investment: Investors can hold fractional ownership in large properties without the responsibility of property management.

🧠 CONSIDERATIONS

DSTs provide limited control over the management of the properties, and decisions are made by the trustee.

Dynasty trust

🎯 PURPOSE

A dynasty trust is designed to hold assets, including real estate, for multiple generations, allowing wealth to be passed down without being subject to estate taxes at each generational transfer.

👥 ADVANTAGES

- Long-term wealth preservation: Real estate assets in a dynasty trust can grow and generate income for several generations
- Estate tax benefits: Assets in the trust can be excluded from the taxable estate of the beneficiaries

🧠 CONSIDERATIONS

The trust must be irrevocable, and once the assets are placed in the trust, the terms cannot be easily changed.

These trust structures offer different levels of control, protection, and tax advantages, and the choice of trust will depend on your goals, estate planning needs, and financial strategy. It bears repeating that it's always advisable to consult with legal and tax professionals when selecting the most appropriate trust structure for real estate investments.

In the end, there are a number of ways to reduce your tax liability and increase asset protection, yet SDIRAs continue to be one of the best. They have a place in every individual's retirement and estate planning.

Chapter 11

SDIRAs and CCIMs

"Self-directed IRAs combined with the expertise of a CCIM
give real estate investors a unique edge. By leveraging
specialized knowledge in commercial real estate, investors
can take their retirement savings to the next level, making
smarter and more informed investment decisions."

—Brandon Turner, author of *The Book on Rental Property Investing*

A Match Made in Financial Heaven?

This chapter explores the synergy between SDIRAs and commercial real estate, highlighting the opportunities they present for both individual investors and commercial real estate professionals. By leveraging the unique benefits of SDIRAs, investors can access a broader range of investment options, diversify their portfolios, and optimize their tax advantages. Understanding how SDIRAs and Certified Commercial Investment Members (CCIMs) complement each other can unlock a world of financial potential. A CCCIM is a recognized expert in the commercial and investment real estate industry.[51] Keep reading to discover how these tools can work together to create win-win scenarios in retirement planning and investment.

In this chapter, I will address the following common questions about SDIRAs and CCIMs:

- Are SDIRAs and commercial real estate a good match?
- How might they complement each other?
- What is the win-win potential for individual investors and commercial real estate professionals?

The Role of CRE in a Retirement Portfolio

Commercial real estate (CRE), or corporate real estate, refers to the real property that a company owns or holds for the purposes of housing its

---

[51] "Certified Commercial Investment Member (CCIM)," National Associations of Realtors, accessed November 25, 2024, https://www.nar.realtor/education/designations-and-certifications/certified-commercial-investment-member-ccim.

operations. The CRE umbrella consists of multiple types of properties and facilities, including offices, warehouses, data centers, and retail spaces, which can all be part of a corporate real estate portfolio. Direct investment in this asset class is often overlooked in individual investment portfolios. This has been especially true in the wake of 2008 and the ensuing rush of investors to snap up single-family rental properties. In view of such information, what place should CRE play in an individual's portfolio?

Asset allocation is often discussed in very general terms. People figure they need stocks, bonds, and real estate to balance out their portfolio, but investors wouldn't just buy one stock, right? A good advisor might recommend multiple types of funds, index funds, and so on. It makes sense to seek diversification in real estate too.

To achieve diversity in the real estate portion of a portfolio, one should incorporate multiple properties in multiple locations and of multiple types. Like stocks, that level of diversification in one's real estate portfolio helps insulate investors from market fluctuations, keeps income consistent, and helps create reliability.

The Benefits of Commercial Real Estate Investments

Commercial real estate investing offers many of the same benefits residential real estate investing does, including the creation of passive income, capital gains, and wealth preservation. Commercial real estate comes in many forms:

- Office buildings
- Industrial property
- Multifamily housing
- Hospitality
- Retail space
- Life sciences*
- Special purpose
- Mixed-use
- Self-storage
- Land

Life sciences in real estate refers to an asset class dedicated to providing both laboratory and office space for tenants involved in the study and development of scientific discoveries. Life sciences spaces can either be built from the ground up or converted from an existing office or industrial building.

Let's review the ways CRE is a safer, more reliable investment than residential real estate. Some advantages or selling points make investing in commercial real estate particularly attractive to long-term investors thinking ahead to retirement and beyond.

LOWER COST PER UNIT

A low per-unit cost is an indicator of efficient production and logistics, which ensures profit is being made per sale. Let's look at multifamily apartment buildings, for example, as well as large parcels of land meant for commercial use, office buildings, and malls. These types of real estate offer lower costs per unit or "door" when compared to several single-family homes. That means achieving more diversification and potentially better yields per dollar invested!

EVEN DEEPER DIVERSIFICATION

Multi-tenant properties offer an additional level of diversification. Contrast a $500,000 single-family home rental with a $500,000 twenty-unit apartment building. If one tenant fails to perform in your single-family home rental, you are out the entire rent amount each month. If one or even five of your apartment tenants don't pay, chances are that you will still break even or, better yet, continue to generate positive passive income while placing new tenants into the open units (once the nonpaying tenants have been evicted).

The second form of deep diversification here is that different property sectors turn through cycles at different times. For example, when residential homes are going through a rough patch, multifamily rentals can do incredibly well. Then, there are small retail shopping centers, which may perform very well in tighter economic times, enjoy longer runs, and bounce back earlier than other property types.

EASE OF MANAGEMENT.

Unlike residential properties, commercial properties often have lease terms of five to ten years. This means investors face lower turnover costs and vacancy rates, ensuring a steady cash flow without the hassle of finding new tenants frequently. Multi-tenant commercial properties also mean consolidating property management. That can considerably reduce management costs and increase net profits.

Warren Buffett said he would love to buy up 200,000 single-family rental homes or more if he could find a way to handle the management. If he couldn't comfortably tackle that, clearly few others would want that task. Instead, Buffett personally took a large stake in a sizable commercial real estate portfolio, highlighting how much easier it is to manage a few large commercial properties compared to hundreds of individual single-family homes.

VALUE-ADD POTENTIAL.

"Value-add" is a term used to describe a property that offers an opportunity to increase cash flow through renovations, rebranding, and/or operational efficiencies. Investing in commercial properties may offer significantly more opportunities to control asset value and improve it. Mineral, oil, access, and timber rights are all a part of this. Marketing and positioning can increase occupancy and rental rates. Adding pads, leasable square feet, and changing up tenants can all increase both cash flow and asset value.

Tax Benefits of Commercial Real Estate Investment

Commercial real estate investment offers a variety of natural tax breaks, including many of the standard breaks of investing in real estate as a whole.

DEPRECIATION

Wear and tear of any improvements made to a property can be depreciated over time on your taxes. Every item has a different depreciation schedule. Some types of commercial real estate even offer accelerated depreciation, which allows for larger tax write-downs in earlier years.

A "write-down" reduces the value of an asset for tax and accounting purposes, but the asset still retains some value. A "write-off" reduces the value of an asset to zero and negates any future value.

This includes manufactured housing and mobile home parks, which can be depreciated over 15 years vs. 27.5 years for residential homes. The PATH Act is the Protecting Americans from Tax Hikes Act of 2015, and it provides various measures designed to protect Americans against identity theft and tax fraud and is still in effect today. This act has also extended and made permanent tax breaks, including faster depreciation of some other types of commercial real estate such as retail property and restaurants, as well as reducing the depreciation on improvements made for tenants from 39 years down to 15 years.[52]

DEDUCTIBLE EXPENSES

There are several deductible expenses to consider in commercial properties. Mortgage interest, property improvements, operating expenses such as property management and marketing, as well as travel and entertainment expenses associated with running a real estate business may be deductible. While the same can hold true for single-family rentals (SFRs), the deductions in a commercial property will be exponential in comparison. This is because commercial properties often have higher costs and more extensive operations than SFRs, leading to a greater number and larger scale of deductible expenses, which can significantly reduce taxable income for investors.

ENERGY-EFFICIENT IMPROVEMENTS

Various tax breaks are available for making energy-efficient improvements to commercial real estate. Some may even be able to negotiate substantial longer-term property tax breaks for rebuilding local communities and redeveloping property that will result in job creation.

QUALIFIED SMALL BUSINESS STOCKS

Investing in some types of qualified small business stocks, in companies that invest in commercial real estate, may yield 100 percent tax-free growth under provisions of the PATH Act.

CHARITABLE DONATIONS

Commercial real estate can also be gifted to charities in a variety of ways to reduce overall tax liability. Up to $100,000 can be gifted from an IRA to offset real estate gains. Real estate investors may also sell property at a discount to charity and deduct that differential. They may gift property outright to a nonprofit, give use of the property, gift property with retained use under a life estate, gift the income but retain the asset, or gift additional property rights such as timber, oil and gas, air rights, or the right to develop as a gift to conservational efforts.

---

[52] Adam Hayes, "Protecting Americans from Tax Hikes (PATH) Act: Definition," *Investopedia*, October 24, 2024, https://www.investopedia.com/terms/p/path-act.asp.

WRITING DOWN DEVALUED PROPERTY

Commercial property values can fluctuate over time. Properties may be damaged by natural forces, terror attacks, or criminal and negligent acts of others. In addition, investments in vehicles such as real estate investment trusts (REITs) can suffer from market volatility or poor management.

In order for investors to write off these losses with their SDIRA custodian and the IRS, they must provide documentation evidencing the new value of the investment. This must be a professional opinion of value from a qualified and independent third party, for example, a licensed property appraiser or unbiased outside auditor.

Commercial properties often have more complex structures and higher values than residential properties, which can make the financial impact of damage or devaluation more significant. However, this also means that when commercial property values fluctuate or decline due to damage, market conditions, or poor management, investors have more opportunities to write down these losses and offset other gains. Unlike residential properties, where damage may lead to limited deductions or require substantial repairs without immediate financial relief, commercial real estate investors can benefit from tax write-offs for depreciation and losses. These write-offs, when properly documented with an independent valuation, provide a way to mitigate financial loss and potentially reduce taxable income, enhancing the overall tax efficiency of commercial real estate investments.

SDIRAs and Commercial Real Estate

An SDIRA is a powerful and necessary tool to aid commercial property investors in maximizing the potential of their investments and minimizing tax exposure. In fact, it is not uncommon for both parties in notable CRE transactions to be LLCs and be using 1031 exchanges or SDIRAs.

A real estate IRA provides investors with another level of legal protection while at the same time providing the benefits of access to direct investment and enjoyment of tax-deferred or tax-free gains. This can easily add up to double-digit savings and bonus gains on each investment and each year. Those compounded gains each year quickly snowball over time.

The law of compounding means that even adding an additional $20,000 per year to investment capital, at a modest 8 percent rate of return, will add an additional $2,265,664.22 to a retirement portfolio over thirty years.

Again, an SDIRA can be used to invest directly in all types of commercial real estate, from industrial to office, retail, and multifamily properties. This IRA can be used to purchase properties and invest in partnerships, development companies, REITs, and commercial loan debt.

Creating Win-Wins for Individual Investors and Commercial Real Estate Professionals

For individual investors looking to maximize their portfolios, partnering with commercial real estate (CRE) professionals who understand the power of SDIRAs can be a game changer. The relationship between investors and CRE professionals offers unique opportunities for both parties to succeed.

There are two key ways this partnership flourishes: investors discover new opportunities for their retirement accounts and CRE professionals introduce their clients to the benefits of self-directed investing.

For individual investors, SDIRAs open up a world of opportunities beyond the stock market, including the ability to invest in commercial real estate. Investors can use SDIRAs to protect their portfolios, maximize returns, and minimize taxes, giving them a competitive edge in the marketplace. By working with knowledgeable CRE professionals, investors gain access to deal flow, expertise, and opportunities that might otherwise remain out of reach.

For real estate professionals, introducing investors to the advantages of SDIRAs can strengthen client relationships, build trust, and foster long-term loyalty. Educating investors on how to leverage SDIRAs for real estate not only enhances their financial outcomes but also increases their buying power and diversification potential. In return, CRE professionals benefit from repeat transactions, referrals, and stronger client networks, resulting in increased business volume and long-term profitability.

As an investor, partnering with CRE professionals who understand SDIRAs allows you to unlock new potential in your portfolio. These professionals act as matchmakers, connecting you with high-quality commercial real estate deals while helping you take full advantage of the tax benefits and flexibility that SDIRAs offer.

Before diving into SDIRA-based real estate investing, it's important to understand the regulations governing these accounts and ensure you're working with reputable custodians. In the next section, we'll cover the key considerations for investors looking to collaborate with CRE professionals and SDIRA custodians to achieve financial success.

Chapter 12

Due Diligence for Investors Using SDIRAs for Real Estate

"Conducting due diligence on the front end is essential, but ensuring thorough due diligence on the back end is equally critical for achieving success and mitigating risk."

The landscape of real estate investing has changed significantly in recent years. With fluctuating inventory and evolving laws, individual investors need to be more informed and empowered than ever. Tools like SDIRAs have made it possible for a broader range of people to invest in real estate, but with this power comes the responsibility of staying vigilant—not only when beginning your investment journey but also as you manage and grow your portfolio.

The Importance of Front-End and Back-End Due Diligence

When investing through an SDIRA, thorough due diligence at both the beginning and throughout the life of your investment is essential. On the front end, you need to carefully evaluate real estate opportunities, understand the market, and ensure that each investment aligns with your retirement goals. However, equally important is the ongoing oversight—regularly reviewing your investments to ensure they remain compliant and continue to grow in line with your expectations.

Action Steps for Due Diligence Before Investing in Real Estate

1. RESEARCH THE MARKET

- Analyze local real estate markets, property values, and rental demand.
- Study economic indicators, such as population growth and job market trends.
- Assess the competition in the area, including the supply and demand for rental or commercial properties.

- The BiggerPockets Market Finder (www.BiggerPockets.com/BookMarket) is a great resource for finding your ideal investing area!

2. EVALUATE THE PROPERTY

- You can search for deals with the BiggerPockets Deal Finder (www.BiggerPockets.com/BookDeals).
- Conduct a physical inspection of the property, checking the structure, roofing, electrical, plumbing, and HVAC systems.
- Obtain a professional property appraisal to determine the fair market value.
- Review the property's history, including repairs, past ownership, and maintenance records.

3. ANALYZE FINANCIALS

- Review the property's income and expenses for the past two to three years.
- Calculate key metrics like ROI, cash flow, and cap rate.
- Estimate future expenses, including maintenance, taxes, and property management fees.
- You can use a BiggerPockets Investment Calculator (www.BiggerPockets.com/BookInvestmentCalculators) to quickly and efficiently analyze a potential real estate investment for profitability.

4. ASSESS ZONING AND LEGAL COMPLIANCE

- Confirm that the property adheres to local zoning laws and regulations.
- Ensure there are no outstanding code violations or legal disputes.
- Review any easements, covenants, or restrictions attached to the property.

5. CHECK TITLE AND OWNERSHIP

- Order a title search to confirm clear ownership, and check for liens or encumbrances.
- Obtain title insurance to protect against potential ownership claims.

6. EVALUATE THE NEIGHBORHOOD

- Visit the property's neighborhood at different times of the day to assess safety, traffic, and amenities.
- Research crime rates, schools, and the overall community quality.
- Evaluate proximity to key amenities like transportation, shopping, and major employers.

7. REVIEW EXISTING LEASES (FOR RENTAL PROPERTIES)

- Examine tenant leases for terms, rent amounts, and tenant histories.
- Verify tenant payment records, and ensure the rents are aligned with market rates.
- Check for security deposits and lease expiration dates.

8. UNDERSTAND FINANCING OPTIONS

- Research nonrecourse loans for IRA investments. You can find an investor-friendly lender at www.BiggerPockets.com/BookLender.
- Compare interest rates, loan terms, and repayment schedules.
- Ensure you understand the down payment and cash reserves required.

9. EVALUATE VALUE-ADD OPPORTUNITIES

- Look for ways to increase the property's value through renovations, upgrades, or operational efficiencies.
- Assess the potential for higher rental rates or tenant improvements.
- Review local regulations for property upgrades, such as energy-efficient improvements or zoning changes.

10. CONSULT PROFESSIONALS

- Hire a real estate attorney to review contracts and ensure compliance with legal requirements.
- Consult a tax advisor to understand the tax implications of the investment, including depreciation and deductions. You can find an investor-friendly tax professional on the BiggerPockets website (www.BiggerPockets.com/BookCPA).

- Consider hiring a property management company if you do not plan to manage the property yourself. You can check out the BiggerPockets property management finder at www.BiggerPockets.com/BookPM to find a property management company that fits your needs.

11. RUN BACKGROUND CHECKS

- Investigate the seller's reputation and past business dealings.
- For partnerships, verify the credentials and experience of potential coinvestors.

12. PREPARE FOR EXIT STRATEGIES

- Consider long-term goals for the property, including holding, selling, or refinancing.
- Assess market conditions to determine the best time to sell or cash out.
- Review your financing terms to ensure flexibility in your exit strategy options.

Ongoing Due Diligence: Staying Compliant and Monitoring Your Investments

Due diligence doesn't end once you've made the investment. Regular oversight is crucial to ensuring your investments continue to grow and remain compliant with SDIRA rules and IRS regulations. It's important to:

- Regularly log into your SDIRA account to review your statements.
- Ensure that your investment returns are properly reflected in your account.
- Monitor the performance of your property, ensuring it continues to meet your financial goals.
- Keep up with SDIRA rules to avoid prohibited transactions, which can result in heavy penalties.

Understanding Self-Directed Real Estate Investments

Investing in real estate through an SDIRA allows you to control your financial future, but it requires a well-thought-out plan aligned with your long-term goals. Here's a suggested expansion plan.

- Start locally: Invest in real estate markets you understand.
- Diversify: As your knowledge grows, consider expanding into regional or national markets, including residential, commercial, and multifamily properties.

Budgeting for Your Real Estate Investments

Like any investment strategy, real estate through an SDIRA requires careful budgeting. Make sure you allocate both time and money for research, due diligence, and property management.

Keep in mind that all expenses related to SDIRA investments must come from the IRA itself, not your personal funds.

Building Your Portfolio with SDIRA Investments

Once you have a strategy in place, you can start building your real estate portfolio. Here are some key steps.

1. Research properties: Use trusted resources like the Bigger-Pockets community to get insights into local markets and available properties.
2. Diversify: Invest in various property types to spread risk, such as residential, commercial, and multifamily units.
3. Leverage your network: Connect with real estate agents, property managers, and financial advisors to help you identify the best investment opportunities.
4. Stay educated: Attend webinars, events like BPCON (which you can learn more about at www.BiggerPockets.com/BookB-PCON), and keep up with market trends to stay ahead of the curve.

Staying Compliant: Legal Considerations for SDIRA Investors

It's important to avoid prohibited transactions, which include using your IRA for personal benefit. For example:

- You can't use IRA funds to buy a property for personal use.
- You can't act as the property manager for SDIRA-owned properties.

Always use a trusted third-party custodian to ensure compliance with IRS rules.

A Cautionary Tale

We encountered an example of what happens when someone does not do their due diligence when investing in a real estate-based asset with their self-directed account.

It started with a phone call from an asset sponsor to our office asking if we allow self-directed investing into unsecured notes. We do. The man on the phone was happy to hear that, and later, we learned why he felt that way.

In the days that followed, his client opened an account with us, and she began the process of funding that account by transferring her funds from the existing custodian. Soon we saw a sum of $500,000 enter her account. Her investment documents arrived shortly after.

At this time, I was away at an industry conference where we were discussing instances of fraud within IRA investing. During that conference, I received a call from my staff regarding the unsecured note investment this investor wished to complete. There were issues—several issues.

Ask yourself, would you make an unsecured note on real estate for $500,000? Probably not. This looked shady, so we took a look at where this person lived. She owned a modest home—so modest it was not typical of an accredited investor.

Keep in mind that a note is a security. In order to offer a security, the asset sponsor must be registered with the SEC in that state, and similarly, the asset must be registered. In order to invest in an asset of this size, the investor would need to be accredited.

I mentioned this suspicious investment to one of the leaders of the conference, who made a call to one of his enforcement contacts.

As an industry, we cannot prevent fraud, but we can report it when we suspect it.

Later, when leaving the conference and driving across I-10 from Arizona to California, my phone rang. It was from the state attorney general's office from the state where this account holder lived. We discussed the situation briefly, and from that point an investigation began.

It was determined that the asset sponsor had previously been incarcerated by the SEC for fraud (for two years).

Imagine if this woman had done her due diligence in advance. If she had merely googled the asset sponsor or his company, the information about his legal record would have been evident. There is another source online called BrokerCheck where you can check out anyone registered with the SEC.

She was lucky. Ultimately, she did not go through with this investment, and we were happy to play a role in preventing a woman in her late fifties from losing her retirement savings to a felon.

Final Thoughts

Investing in real estate through an SDIRA can be a powerful strategy for building wealth. By following the steps for due diligence—both before and after making an investment—you can reduce risks, stay compliant with IRS regulations, and grow your retirement savings. Take advantage of the resources available to you, such as the Bigger-Pockets community (www.BiggerPockets.com/Forums51Book), and continue to educate yourself on best practices for SDIRA investing. This proactive approach will set you up for long-term success.

Chapter 13

IRA Administrators

"Your IRA administrator plays a crucial role in your investing journey. Finding one that aligns with your goals and values can be the difference between a frustrating experience and a seamless path to building wealth."

—Brandon Turner, author of *The Book on Rental Property Investing*

Finding IRA Services Firms

Finding self-directed IRA services companies and custodians is not that difficult. Here are some ideas:

- Reach out to the Retirement Industry Trust Association, which you can find at www.ritaus.org
- Search Google
- Ask for referrals
- Turn to industry platforms like BiggerPockets

Selecting a Great IRA Services Partner

What is the best way for you to select a great IRA service provider?

REVIEWS

Check out the online reviews. What are others saying about their service? How many complaints do they have in relation to the volume of business they are doing? Companies may never be able to stop frivolous and malicious complaints, but check how they handle bad reviews and complaints.

Channels to check for reviews and feedback include Yelp, Google, and the Better Business Bureau.

EVALUATE

To determine a company's effort and investment, look for signs such as a professional, up-to-date website; active membership in reputable industry associations; and a strong commitment to educating others through resources like webinars, articles, or seminars. Green flags include positive testimonials from trusted sources and recommendations from well-respected professionals in the field. Conversely, red flags might include a lack of transparency, outdated or poorly maintained websites, and minimal engagement in industry education or associations. Always verify the credibility of their references and affiliations to ensure you're partnering with a reliable and reputable organization.

INTERVIEW THEM

Despite all the tips mentioned above, assessing a company or an individual professional can still be challenging, as this holds true across all areas of the real estate and financial industries. One of the most effective ways to vet service providers is to interview them directly. This can be done over the phone, through online video calls, or in person. Prepare a list of key questions in advance to ensure you cover all important topics. During the conversation, evaluate their responses to gauge their competence, ensure their values align with yours, and check that their costs are competitive. This approach will help you find a reliable SDIRA firm that meets your needs.

Interview Questions

Here is a list of questions to ask when interviewing an SDIRA firm to ensure they are competent and a good fit for your needs:

What types of SDIRAs do you offer?

This question helps you understand the range of services provided and whether they align with your investment goals.

How long have you been in business, and what is your experience with SDIRAs?

Understanding the firm's history and experience can give you confidence in their ability to manage your investments effectively.

What fees do you charge for account setup, maintenance, and transactions?

Transparency about fees is crucial to avoid unexpected costs and to ensure the firm's pricing is competitive.

Can you provide references or testimonials from current or past clients?

References can provide insight into the firm's reliability, customer service, and overall performance.

What types of investments can I make with an SDIRA through your firm?

Confirm that the firm allows the specific types of investments you are interested in, such as real estate, private placements, or precious metals.

What processes do you have in place to assure compliance with IRS rules and regulations?

A competent firm should have robust compliance processes to help you avoid prohibited transactions and other regulatory pitfalls.

How do you handle customer service, and what is your response time for client inquiries?

Excellent customer service and prompt responses are indicators of a reliable firm.

What educational resources do you offer to help me understand my SDIRA options and responsibilities?

A good firm will provide educational materials, webinars, or seminars to help you make informed decisions.

Are you members of any professional organizations or industry associations?

Membership in reputable organizations can indicate a commitment to industry standards and ongoing education.

How secure is your platform and data management?

Ensure that the firm has strong security measures to protect your personal and financial information.

What is your process for handling investments and distributions?

Understanding their processes will give you an idea of how easy it is to manage your investments and access your funds.

Can you walk me through the account opening process?

This question helps you understand the steps involved and how long it will take to get started.

> **How do you handle communication and updates regarding my account?**
>
> Regular communication and updates are vital for staying informed about your investments and any changes that may affect them. Understanding how the firm manages potential conflicts can help you assess their integrity and commitment to your best interests.

Asking these questions will help you gauge the firm's expertise, reliability, and alignment with your investment goals, ensuring you choose a competent SDIRA provider.

Ensure competence

The IRA services space is highly attractive to finance professionals, but not everyone has true depth and length of experience. How much have they been managing in terms of assets for other clients? How long have they been in business? Can they spot issues others are overlooking? What quality control and checks do they have in place to keep you safe?

Assess values

Does this firm share your values? Retirement planning is a long-term game and a very important and personal one. You will want to work with an ethical company that shares your values, can aid with your personal approach and strategy, is highly proactive about educating you in ways to protect your investments, plus suggests things to consider regarding tax liability and staying ahead of regulatory changes.

Compare competitive costs

Unchecked and uncompetitive fees and charges can really take a bite out of your gains, retirement nest egg, and lifestyle and succession plans. Make sure you understand the costs involved, how to minimize them, and where to find the best balance of service and expense.

The Costs Involved with Self-Directed Retirement Accounts

In the book *Money: How to Master the Game*, Tony Robbins (along with the nation's leading financial experts) reveals just how cloudy fee structures are when it comes to traditional 401(k)s and IRAs. Most individuals have absolutely no idea how much they are really paying across multiple levels of charges, commissions, and management fees.

Ultimately, that can easily cost investors hundreds of thousands if not millions of dollars over the years. Shaving just a few points off of those fees that can make all the difference in retiring well.

In comparison, the administrative fees for SDIRAs can be very straightforward. New account setup fees can start at just $50. There may be modest annual fees. There may be sliding scale management fees based upon the size of a portfolio, or there may be small transactional fees ranging from $5 to over $200.

Potential SDIRA related fees include:
- Setup
- Wires
- Check writing
- Copies of tax documents
- Closing an IRA account
- Courier service
- Return check fees
- Changing account types
- Storage fees for precious metals

The Process of Investing Through an SDIRA
As with everything in life and business, there is a process to follow when investing through an SDIRA.

1. Open or rollover an existing retirement account.
2. Begin funding your account.
3. Review and select investments.
4. Have your administrator review the documents to make sure you are in compliance.
5. Instruct the administrator to fund the investment or use your IRA LLC checkbook (outlined in Chapter 17).
6. Obtain your annual tax documents and save on taxes.
7. Reinvest your gains and savings to snowball your nest egg and passive income.
8. Begin taking minimum withdrawals once you hit the mandatory age.

WHAT THE CUSTODIAN DOES

The IRA services firm acts as a custodian and administrator for your retirement funds. It is their responsibility to safeguard funds, which are sitting as a nonvested balance. They ought to vet each investment and the paperwork to ensure compliance and preservation of tax-saving benefits. At your request and on your behalf, they will execute the funding of your investment choices. As needed and requested, they will send checks to pay various management-related fees for investments, such as property maintenance, invoices, or property taxes. Then, this provider will provide your annual tax documents and facilitate withdrawals as requested.

WHAT YOU AS THE ACCOUNT HOLDER DO

The most important thing to know is that SDIRA services (service providers) do not select, suggest, or pick investments for you. In fact, law prohibits them from this. If they do, or if they commingle promoting investments and IRA services, count that as a massive red flag.

They will be there to review your strategy and specific investments and tactics for compliance and to ensure you remain covered by this tax-saving umbrella, but they shouldn't cross the line to advising on investment choices or speculating on performance.

It is up to you to fund your account, to look for and identify the investments you want your money to go into. When it comes to real estate investments, you will select your own property managers or fund managers and direct related payments unless delegated to someone else.

You make the calls on when to get in, when to sell investments, and when to restructure your portfolio. You will take your tax documents to your personal accountant or tax preparer to claim your breaks and deductions.

What to Expect from a Good IRA Administrator: Investor's Perspective

As an investor using an SDIRA, the role of your IRA administrator is crucial to your success. When selecting an administrator, there are certain expectations and standards you should demand to ensure your investments are managed effectively and securely. Here's a guide to help you understand what to expect from a good IRA administrator.

EXCEPTIONAL CUSTOMER SERVICE

You should expect your IRA administrator to prioritize customer service. This means having access to knowledgeable and responsive staff who are available to answer your questions and provide guidance.

Good customer service goes beyond just being friendly; it involves clear communication and a commitment to ensuring you fully understand your account, the rules, and any potential risks associated with your investments.

A good administrator will take the time to explain complex topics and repeat the information as many times as necessary until you are comfortable. As an investor, you have the right to demand clarity and transparency at every step.

RELIABLE AND HONEST GUIDANCE

Although IRA administrators are not allowed to give specific investment advice, they should provide solid information that helps keep your investments within legal boundaries. This may include informing you about prohibited transactions, contribution limits, and other IRS rules that apply to your SDIRA.

The guidance you receive may not always align with what you hope to hear, but it should be designed to protect you from costly mistakes. A good administrator will prioritize your long-term financial safety over short-term gains, ensuring your investments remain compliant with IRS regulations.

TRANSPARENCY AND ACCOUNTABILITY

Transparency is a hallmark of any trustworthy IRA administrator. You should have a clear understanding of the fees, services, and processes involved in managing your account. Look for administrators who are up front about their costs and willing to explain where your money is going.

A good administrator will be willing to answer your questions openly and without hesitation. They should also be proactive in addressing any concerns you have about your account, providing regular updates, and keeping you informed about changes in tax laws or regulations that could impact your investments.

COMMITMENT TO CONTINUOUS TRAINING AND EDUCATION

The landscape of self-directed retirement accounts is constantly evolving, with new laws, IRS guidelines, and investment opportunities emerging regularly. A good IRA administrator will be committed to staying ahead of these changes by regularly training their staff and ensuring they are well informed.

As an investor, you benefit from working with a team that is always up to date on the latest regulations. This reduces your risk of running afoul of tax laws or missing out on potential opportunities to maximize your investments.

DEPENDABLE AND LONG-TERM FOCUS

A good IRA administrator will have a sustainable business model with a long-term outlook, ensuring that they can consistently serve your needs for years to come. This stability is essential for the security of your retirement funds. When choosing an administrator, it's important to research their history, reputation, and financial standing.

You want to work with an administrator who has a proven track record of handling IRAs responsibly and staying ahead of the curve when it comes to changes in the industry.

NEUTRALITY AND NONCOMPETITION

Your IRA administrator should remain neutral and impartial when it comes to your investments. They should not push specific investment products or services, as their role is purely administrative, not advisory. Be cautious of any administrators who seem to have conflicts of interest or who try to steer you toward certain investment types for their own gain.

A good administrator will not compete with you or your financial goals, and their focus should be entirely on facilitating your chosen investments in a compliant and efficient manner.

POSITIVE REVIEWS AND RECOMMENDATIONS

Before committing to an IRA administrator, it's wise to seek out reviews and recommendations from other investors. A well-regarded administrator will have a strong reputation within the community and be known for their reliability and professionalism.

Ask your peers about their experiences with various administrators, and consider this feedback when making your decision. Knowing that others have had positive outcomes can give you peace of mind as you entrust your retirement funds to an administrator.

Choosing the right IRA administrator is a critical decision that can significantly impact your ability to manage and grow your retirement savings. By focusing on customer service, transparency, honesty, and long-term stability, you can ensure that you're partnering with a firm that has your best interests in mind. A good IRA administrator will act as a trusted ally in helping you navigate the complexities of SDIRAs, keeping your investments compliant and on track toward your financial goals.

Chapter 14

Creating an Action Plan

"Building a secure retirement doesn't happen by accident—
it requires a clear, actionable plan. The sooner you take
control and map out your steps, the closer you'll get
to financial freedom."

—Kathy Fettke, author of *Retire Rich with Rentals* and
coauthor of *Scaling Smart*

Creating a Personal Investment Action Plan

This is a great time to take a moment to reevaluate your own personal retirement plan and investments. Do you have a dedicated retirement portfolio? Is it optimized to deliver on your desired goals and lifestyle for retirement and beyond? If you are not already using a self-directed retirement account, how might one help increase your yields, capital gains, and the velocity at which you are building a nest egg and passive income streams? If you are behind on retirement planning, how might starting a plan like this reduce your income tax bill next year (and every year) while making up for lost time and providing peace of mind?

Start or revisit your retirement and investment plan now.

Put it on paper, or at least have your plan in black and white stored in the cloud. Start planning and refining your plan by:

- Reviewing and setting new goals.
- Talking to existing investment professionals about using SDIRAs.
- Speaking with your accountant about the tax benefits for you.
- Meeting with an SDIRA expert.
- Creating your strategy to choose the assets that best suit you.

Start with Strategy, by Dave Meyer, is a great resource that gives you a practical framework to craft and execute your personalized real estate plan. You can find the book at www.BiggerPockets.com/ReadSWS.

Creating an Action Plan to Incorporate SDIRAs into Your Investment Strategy

Once you've taken care of your personal financial planning, the next step is to enhance your investment approach by incorporating the benefits of SDIRAs. This action plan will help you strategically integrate SDIRAs into your broader investment portfolio, maximizing your returns and adding valuable diversification.

Here's what your action plan should include.

1. Choose an IRA service provider: Research and select reputable SDIRA custodians or service providers who can facilitate your self-directed investments and offer long-term support.
2. Understand SDIRA rules and benefits: Familiarize yourself with the specific rules and benefits of SDIRAs, such as the ability to invest in alternative assets like real estate, tax deferral or tax-free growth through Roth accounts, and the opportunities for portfolio diversification.
3. Identify opportunities: Pinpoint which types of investments—such as real estate, private lending, or other alternative assets—best suit your investment goals and align with SDIRA regulations.
4. Budget plan: Determine how much of your investment capital you want to allocate toward SDIRA investments and consider the potential for long-term growth, diversification, and tax savings.
5. Review and adjust: As with any strategy, it's important to review your plan periodically, ensuring it stays aligned with your broader financial goals and adjusts to any market changes.

By taking a proactive approach to incorporating SDIRAs, you position yourself to unlock new investment opportunities and maximize the advantages of tax-advantaged growth. This approach also helps ensure your retirement savings are diversified beyond traditional stocks and bonds. Take the time to create a well-structured plan, making SDIRA investments a core part of your long-term financial strategy.

Any good investor action plan includes consultation from professionals and other resources to ensure you're maximizing the potential of this powerful investment tool.

Chapter 15

The Power of the Solo 401(k)— Building Wealth with Your Retirement Plan

"The solo 401(k) is one of the most powerful tools available to self-employed investors. With higher contribution limits and greater flexibility, it's a game changer for those looking to accelerate their wealth-building through retirement planning."

—David Greene, author of *Buy, Rehab, Rent, Refinance, Repeat*

Do You Qualify for a Solo 401(k)?

If you're a small business owner or self-employed, a solo 401(k) could be the key to taking your retirement investing to the next level. Designed specifically for those who are the only employee of their business (or just you and your spouse), this plan offers powerful tax advantages, investment flexibility, and total control over your savings. If this sounds like you, then you might be eligible to set up an individual 401(k), also known as a solo 401(k), and start maximizing your financial future.

This chapter will dive into the essential details you need to know about the solo 401(k), from self-directing your investments to understanding contribution and distribution rules, the Roth component, and funding strategies. Designed specifically for solo entrepreneurs or self-employed individuals without employees, the solo 401(k) differs from traditional 401(k) plans, which are built for larger companies with multiple employees. By the end of this chapter, you'll also learn how to set up and manage your own solo 401(k) plan.

WHAT IS A SOLO 401(K)?

A solo 401(k), also known as a one-participant 401(k), is designed for businesses that employ only the business owner and their spouse. This plan works in the same way as a traditional 401(k) but with unique advantages that cater to entrepreneurs and self-employed individuals.

In the past few years, the solo 401(k) has gone through several changes, making it even more powerful for retirement investing. As an experienced investor or business owner, you may be looking for ways to optimize your retirement contributions, minimize taxes, and grow your wealth over time. The solo 401(k) allows you to do just that with features such as higher contribution limits and the ability to invest in a wide range of assets through self-direction.

ADVANTAGES OF A SOLO 401(K)

The solo 401(k) plan comes with numerous advantages that make it one of the best retirement savings vehicles for self-employed individuals.

- High contribution limits: One of the primary reasons entrepreneurs choose a solo 401(k) is the high contribution limits. As both the employee and the employer, you can contribute in two ways:
  - Employee contributions: As an employee, you can contribute up to $23,000 in 2024 (or $30,000 if you're 50 or older through catch-up contributions).
  - Employer contributions: As the employer, you can contribute up to 25 percent of your compensation, allowing for a total contribution of up to $69,000 ($73,500 with catch-up contributions) in 2024. This flexibility lets you maximize your contributions and grow your retirement savings faster than with other retirement accounts.
- Tax benefits: Depending on how you structure your solo 401(k), you can take advantage of tax-deferred growth, or you can opt for tax-free growth by utilizing the Roth component (more on this below). This allows for strategic tax planning, giving you more control over your tax burden in the short and long term.
- Self-direction: With a solo 401(k), you have the option to self-direct your investments. This means you are not limited to traditional investments like stocks, bonds, and mutual funds. Instead, you can invest in alternative assets such as real estate, private equity, tax liens, promissory notes, and more. Self-directing your solo 401(k) gives you greater flexibility to invest in opportunities that align with your overall investment strategy.

- Loan provision: A unique feature of the solo 401(k) is the ability to borrow from your account. You can take out a loan of up to 50 percent of the account value, with a maximum loan amount of $50,000. The loan must be repaid over five years with interest, but the principal and interest are paid back into your account, allowing you to use the money while continuing to grow your retirement savings.
- No RMDs for Roth solo 401(k)s: Another significant advantage of the solo 401(k) is that Roth contributions are not subject to required minimum distributions (RMDs) when you reach age 73 (as of 2024). This means you can let your Roth solo 401(k) continue to grow tax free for as long as you like, without being forced to withdraw funds.

SELF-DIRECTING YOUR SOLO 401(K)

With Solo 401(k) plans, you act as the trustee. You have the responsibility and signing authority to sign various investment-related documents to ensure the plan complies with the guidelines set by the IRS and other regulations. The extent of your authority will depend on the specific plan rules, which can be found in the plan documents.

Self-directing a solo 401(k) allows you to expand your investment options beyond traditional stocks, bonds, and mutual funds. By choosing a custodian that offers self-directed accounts, you can invest in a wide range of alternative assets, including:

- Real estate: Many solo 401(k) account holders invest in rental properties, commercial real estate, or even raw land. Real estate can provide both long-term appreciation and passive income.
- Private equity: You can use your solo 401(k) to invest in privately held companies, whether through direct ownership or as part of an investment group.
- Precious metals: Investing in gold, silver, or other precious metals is a popular option for those looking to hedge against inflation.
- Cryptocurrency: For more adventurous investors, cryptocurrency is an option, although this asset class can be volatile and may require special handling.

- Tax liens and promissory notes: Solo 401(k) account holders can also invest in tax liens or act as a lender by investing in promissory notes.

Self-directing your solo 401(k) allows you to invest in assets you understand best, offering you the potential for greater returns. However, self-directed investments also come with risks, so it's important to perform thorough due diligence before making any decisions.

CONTRIBUTION AND DISTRIBUTION RULES

Understanding the contribution and distribution rules for a solo 401(k) is critical to taking full advantage of the plan's benefits.

ROTH VS. TRADITIONAL CONTRIBUTIONS

You can choose to contribute to a traditional solo 401(k), where contributions are tax deferred, or a Roth solo 401(k), where contributions are made with after-tax dollars, but qualified distributions are tax-free.

- Traditional solo 401(k): Contributions are made on a pretax basis, reducing your taxable income in the year of contribution. However, you will pay taxes when you take distributions in retirement.
- Roth solo 401(k): Contributions are made with after-tax dollars, meaning there is no immediate tax deduction. However, all future qualified distributions are tax free, making this an excellent option for those expecting to be in a higher tax bracket during retirement.

DISTRIBUTIONS

Like other retirement plans, distributions from a solo 401(k) can begin penalty free at age 59 ½. Distributions taken before that age may be subject to a 10 percent early withdrawal penalty unless they qualify for an exception (such as hardship withdrawals).

If you contribute to a traditional solo 401(k), you will need to start taking required minimum distributions (RMDs) at age 73, unless you are still working. However, Roth contributions are not subject to RMDs, which gives you greater flexibility to manage your retirement income.

THE ROTH COMPONENT OF A SOLO 401(K)

One of the most powerful features of a solo 401(k) is the ability to contribute to a Roth component. By making Roth contributions, you forego the immediate tax deduction but gain the benefit of tax-free distributions in retirement. This can be particularly beneficial if you expect to be in a higher tax bracket when you retire or want to avoid RMDs.

For many business owners, the flexibility of having both traditional and Roth options within their solo 401(k) offers an ideal way to diversify tax strategies. You can even split your contributions between both components, depending on your short- and long-term financial goals.

SETTING UP A SOLO 401(K): STEP-BY-STEP GUIDE

Setting up a solo 401(k) may seem complex, but the process can be straightforward if you follow these steps:

1. Choose a plan provider: Research and choose a plan provider that offers the features and investment options you want, including the ability to self-direct your plan. Many financial institutions and specialized solo 401(k) custodians offer these services.
2. Draft your plan document: You'll need to create the official plan document that governs your solo 401(k). This document outlines the rules of your plan, including contribution limits, distribution rules, and investment options. Often your plan provider will create a plan document and provide updates when IRS rules change.
3. Obtain an Employer Identification Number (EIN): You will need an EIN from the IRS to establish your solo 401(k). This is a straightforward process that can be completed online. Again, your plan provider may provide this service for you.
4. Open a solo 401(k) bank account: Unless your plan provider also serves as custodian of your solo(k) funds, you will need to open a bank or brokerage account in the name of the solo 401(k) trust. This account will be used to receive contributions and make investments.
5. Start contributing: Begin making contributions to your solo 401(k) based on the contribution limits discussed earlier. You can also roll over funds from other qualified retirement accounts.

6.   Invest your funds: If you have opted for a self-directed solo 401(k), you can start investing your funds in the assets of your choice.

Summary

The solo 401(k) is a powerful retirement savings plan tailored for self-employed individuals and small business owners with no employees, offering high contribution limits, tax benefits, and the ability to self-direct investments into a wide range of assets such as real estate and private equity. With contributions possible as both employer and employee, the plan allows for flexible funding and strategic tax planning, including Roth contributions for tax-free retirement distributions. The plan also offers the option to borrow from the account and provides greater control over investment choices. Setting up a solo 401(k) involves selecting a plan provider, creating a plan document, obtaining an EIN, and opening a designated account for contributions and investments. This plan is ideal for entrepreneurs looking to maximize their retirement savings and grow wealth through diverse investment opportunities.

eQRP vs. Solo 401(k): Breaking Down the Difference

IS EQRP JUST A FANCY TERM FOR A SOLO 401(K)?

If you've come across the term Enhanced Qualified Retirement Plan (eQRP) and wondered how it compares to the solo 401(k), you're not alone. Many experts in the industry argue that the eQRP is simply a rebrand or marketing term for a self-directed solo 401(k). While there are subtle distinctions that eQRP promoters highlight—such as additional creditor protection—the core IRS statutory rules apply to both.

Whether a self-employed retirement plan like a solo 401(k) or eQRP is protected from creditors depends on the participant's state of residence, not the plan's specific terminology (eQRP). In states such as Colorado, Florida, Texas, and Idaho, these self-employed plans receive full protection from creditors.

For practical purposes, eQRP and solo 401(k) plans serve a very similar function, and for self-employed individuals looking to maximize retirement savings, both are excellent options. Let's break down the key similarities and differences between these two plans to understand their nuances.

What Is a Solo 401(k)?

To recap, a solo 401(k), also known as a one-participant 401(k), is a qualified retirement plan designed for self-employed individuals and small business owners who have no full-time employees other than their spouse. Solo 401(k)s offer high contribution limits, self-directed investment opportunities, tax advantages, and the ability to borrow from the account. They are favored by those who want control over their retirement funds and the flexibility to invest in both traditional and alternative assets like real estate, private equity, and even cryptocurrency.

What Is an eQRP?

The eQRP, or Enhanced Qualified Retirement Plan, is a concept popularized by specific companies and marketed as an upgrade to the solo 401(k). Essentially, it functions similarly to a self-directed solo 401(k), allowing for diverse investments, Roth contributions, and checkbook control. However, proponents of the eQRP emphasize enhanced creditor protection and the ability to handle larger, more complex financial strategies, such as rolling over funds from multiple retirement accounts with fewer limitations.

KEY SIMILARITIES BETWEEN EQRP AND SOLO 401(K)

- Self-employment requirement: Both plans are designed for self-employed individuals or small business owners without employees. To qualify for either, you must have earned income from self-employment.
- High contribution limits: Both the solo 401(k) and eQRP allow for high annual contributions—up to $69,000 (or $73,500 with catch-up contributions) for 2024, depending on your income and age. This is significantly higher than the contribution limits for IRAs.
- Self-directed investments: Both plans allow for a wide range of investment options, including traditional assets like stocks and bonds, as well as alternative investments such as real estate, precious metals, tax liens, and private company shares.
- Roth component: Both the eQRP and solo 401(k) allow for Roth contributions, enabling participants to contribute after-tax dollars and enjoy tax-free distributions in retirement.

- Checkbook control: Both plans offer checkbook control, meaning participants can make investment decisions without going through a custodian. This feature is particularly appealing to those looking to invest in alternative assets.
- Creditor protection: Both plans offer a degree of creditor protection, though the extent of this protection depends on state laws and plan design.

KEY DIFFERENCES BETWEEN EQRP AND SOLO 401(K)

- Marketing vs. actual structure: The eQRP is largely a marketing term for a self-directed solo 401(k), but it's advertised as having stronger creditor protection. However, the additional protections typically depend on state law or plan structure rather than being inherent to the eQRP term itself.
- Creditor protection claims: Proponents of the eQRP claim that it offers more robust creditor protection compared to the solo 401(k). However, the truth is that whether a retirement plan is protected from creditors depends largely on state laws. In some states, solo 401(k) plans already offer substantial creditor protection, making the eQRP differentiation less significant in practice.
- LLC and plan setup: While a solo 401(k) can offer checkbook control directly, the eQRP is sometimes structured with an LLC or C corporation setup to enhance protection from creditors. This indirect protection involves setting up the plan to invest through a legal entity (like an LLC), which can offer a shield against claims. However, this structure can also be applied to a solo 401(k).
- Rollover flexibility: The eQRP is often marketed as offering easier and more flexible rollovers from other retirement accounts, such as traditional IRAs, 401(k)s, or 403(b)s. However, this is also possible with a solo 401(k), so the real difference lies in how these options are presented and marketed.
- Ability to hire employees: While the solo 401(k) is designed for businesses with no full-time employees, the eQRP may allow greater flexibility if you eventually want to hire

employees. However, at that point, a traditional 401(k) or another type of qualified retirement plan might be more appropriate.

- Filing requirements: Both plans have filing requirements once they reach certain thresholds in asset value. For example, when the total plan assets exceed $250,000, the solo 401(k) must file Form 5500-EZ. In the case of rollovers and transfers, the forms and processes are similar, with slight differences in reporting based on the plan design.

Common Misconceptions

A common misconception is that the eQRP provides inherently better protection or flexibility than a solo 401(k). In reality, both plans fall under the same IRS rules, and any differences largely depend on how the plans are structured and the specific legal strategies used rather than a fundamental distinction between the two. The term "eQRP" is more of a branding effort to differentiate from the traditional solo 401(k), but the core features and benefits remain quite similar.

Which Is Right for You?

For most self-employed individuals, a solo 401(k) offers ample flexibility, high contribution limits, and the ability to self-direct investments. If your primary focus is on investing in alternative assets and maximizing retirement savings, the solo 401(k) is likely sufficient. However, if you are particularly concerned about creditor protection or anticipate hiring employees in the future, you may want to explore the eQRP structure or similar strategies. Ultimately, the decision between an eQRP and a solo 401(k) comes down to personal preference, the complexity of your financial situation, and how much you value the additional costs and legal and structural features marketed under the eQRP umbrella. Both plans can serve as powerful tools for retirement savings and investment growth. They are both exactly the same for tax purposes.

Chapter 16

Investing with Your SDIRA

"With a Self-Directed IRA, your investment choices aren't limited by traditional accounts. It's a tool that puts you in the driver's seat, giving you the freedom to grow your wealth beyond stocks and bonds."

—Scott Trench, author of *Set for Life*

Once you have your SDIRA opened and funded, it's time to invest. You can invest your IRA dollars in anything except life insurance contracts and collectibles. Keep in mind the rules about prohibited transactions when investing.

Prohibited transactions are fully discussed in IRS Code (IRC) 4975. Some of the more common investment transactions with an SDIRA include real estate, notes (both secured and unsecured), private placements (subscriptions into nonpublicly traded stock), wholesale transactions, and precious metals, just to name a few.

Also common are IRA-owned LLCs, whereby the account holder is the manager and the IRA is the sole member. This is often referred to as a "checkbook IRA" since the account holder has the check-writing authority of IRA funds as the manager of the LLC.

Regardless of the investment type, the account holder will provide the supporting investment docs with their Direction of Investment (DOI) form. We will further discuss some of the more common types of investments in this chapter.

Titling for all investments should be in the name of: <First Name Last Name>, legal owner via non-trust custodial IRA with AET. This titling allows you, the account holder, to sign investment documents for your IRA. However, it should be noted that you cannot title documents in your personal name, nor can you assign a contract to your IRA.

Titling may also look like: "Custodian for the Benefit Of John Doe, Account Holder Account #XXXX." In this case, the custodian would sign the investment documents.

Purchasing real estate with your IRA is much the same process as purchasing from personal funds with the main exception being how titling is held. All real estate transactions and investments in general should be arms-length transactions. To fund the earnest money deposit and/or the balance due for settlement, the account holder will complete a DOI form instructing the IRA to fund said investment.

Along with the completed DOI form, you should provide a copy of the related purchase contract along with a closing statement from the settlement agent for funding of balance due for settlement. The custodian will stamp the contract at time of funding the transaction, thereby acknowledging the transaction to be an IRA asset.

Promissory notes, both secured and unsecured, are another common investment we see. Investing in promissory notes can be achieved via a new note or the purchase of an existing note. A secured note would require a deed of trust, or mortgage, to be provided along with the note. Whether the collateral/security document is to be a deed of trust or mortgage will depend on the state the loan collateral is located in. You can learn more about note investing in *Real Estate Note Investing: Using Mortgage Notes to Passively and Massively Increase Your Income* by Dave Van Horn (www.BiggerPockets.com/ReadRENoteInvesting).

If the note is to be unsecured, the IRA would require a hold harmless letter to be signed by you, acknowledging the higher risk of loss involved in an unsecured note. Should you purchase an existing note, you would also provide an assignment from the seller to the IRA. If purchasing a note for less than face value, a bill of sale between the IRA and the seller will be needed, outlining the price to be paid for the note by the IRA. Often, an amortization schedule may be required when purchasing an existing note for less than face value. SDIRAs can also invest in nonpublicly traded stock, also referred to as a "private placement." Investing into a private placement is typically done through a subscription agreement.

In some cases, especially with companies raising capital through only a handful of investors, the company may only use/provide an operating agreement from the asset sponsor with a member ledger outlining the investors and initial capital contributions. In other cases, both a subscription agreement and an operating agreement are needed to complete your private placement investment. In either case, the company you intend to invest into with your IRA will provide the documents needed to complete the investment. A DOI form will also be needed, directing the IRA to make said investment.

Wholesaling is another type of investment that can be completed through your IRA. Wholesaling typically involves real estate in that the account holder enters into a contract on behalf of the IRA to purchase a property. However, the contract is then assigned to another purchaser to complete the purchase of the property. Of course, the idea here is that the IRA receives a wholesaling fee, or finder's fee, for the transaction. Much like a real estate transaction, the account holder will provide the purchase contract, DOI form, assignment (to assign the contract from IRA to new buyer), wholesaling contract/bill of sale, along with an authorization to execute form requesting that the IRA stamp the contract to acknowledge the pending investment. Upon completion of the buyer's purchase of the property, the IRA receives its wholesaling fee at time of settlement from the closing agent.

For those account holders who wish to have direct control, including check-writing authority over their investments, there is the IRA-owned LLC. As briefly mentioned earlier, an IRA-owned LLC is an LLC entity wherein the IRA is the sole member, and the account holder is its manager. This setup allows the account holder to have direct check-writing abilities alone. With such control comes great responsibility. Since IRA compliance is only involved in the initial funding of the LLC, any subsequent investments made under the LLC are not subject to IRA review.

In other words, the asset of the IRA is the LLC. The asset of the LLC is all subsequent investments that are then made under the LLC's umbrella. For the custodial compliance department to approve and fund the LLC, they generally need copies of:

1. A manager-signed operating agreement with member ledger showing the IRA as sole member and the amount of initial contribution to be made from the IRA.
2. An EIN acceptance letter (this is the letter issued by the IRS confirming issuance of the company's tax ID number).
3. A hold harmless letter signed by the account holder (account holder agrees to abide by IRC 4975 guidelines governing prohibited transactions).
4. The completed DOI form.

Precious metals can also be held in your IRA. Unlike some publicly traded funds that merely hedge the prices of gold or silver, or other metals for that matter, your IRA can physically hold precious metals.

However, not all metals can be held. Fineness requirements of precious metals restrict those metals that can be held to a purity fineness of .9999. Metals are stored in a warehouse, such as the Delaware Depository.

To complete a metals investment with your IRA generally requires:

1. An invoice/bill of sale between the IRA and metals dealer of your choosing (the invoice/bill of sale should outline the metals to be purchased and price to be paid by the IRA).
2. A packing slip completed by the dealer.
3. A completed DOI form from you.

There are many other types of investments that can be made from your IRA. Some of those not covered here may include, but are not limited to, tax lien certificates, oil and gas investments, judgments/structured settlements, accounts receivable, and equipment leasing.

All investments are subject to IRA compliance review. That said, not all investments will be deemed administratively feasible for the IRA to hold. This is a term used in the industry to indicate the investment will not be held in custody by the custodian for a variety of reasons. One example of an asset that is not administratively feasible would be Bitcoin. Cryptocurrencies, unlike precious metals, cannot be physically held in custody by the custodian. Accordingly, our account holders cannot invest in such currency. Not all custodians share this viewpoint.

Other investments that are deemed not administratively feasible are those into companies dealing in the marijuana trade. This may change over time. Right now, even though such businesses are becoming popular in more and more states that have legalized the trade, federal law trumps state law. It is federal law, not state law, that oversees legislation pertaining to IRAs and other qualified retirement plans.

Chapter 17

Checkbook Control LLCs

"Checkbook control LLCs give you unparalleled speed and flexibility in managing your self-directed IRA investments. But with great power comes great responsibility—knowing the rules is key to avoiding costly mistakes."

—John Hyre, tax attorney and self-directed IRA expert

A common question for real estate investors is "Which entity should I use?" This can be a challenging decision, as there is a lot of misinformation about asset protection and entity structures. In the context of IRA-owned LLCs, this issue becomes even more complex. Many investors encounter misleading advice, particularly from those promoting "checkbook LLCs" or "IRA-owned LLCs" without a deep understanding of IRA laws.

Two primary concerns arise:

- Severe consequences of prohibited transactions: Prohibited transactions within an IRA can lead to disastrous financial consequences, often resulting in significant tax penalties and the disqualification of the IRA.
- Misinformation from sellers: Many promoters of IRA-owned LLCs, often referred to as checkbook LLCs, lack sufficient knowledge of IRA rules. They tend to oversimplify complex legal cases and offer generic templates under the guise of personalized service, which can be risky for investors.

Important Note: Prohibited Transactions

The most critical rules governing IRAs are the prohibited transaction rules as outlined in IRC Section 4975. Even a small prohibited transaction can destroy an entire IRA, leading to tax liabilities and penalties that could deplete the account. For instance, a minor loan from an IRA to a family member could result in the complete distribution of the IRA's assets, with severe tax and penalty consequences. Here is an example of a prohibited transaction with negative consequences. Say an IRA worth $1,666,667 lends just $1 to the IRA owner's mother, which is a prohibited transaction. This results in the entire IRA being distributed and subject to taxes and penalties, leading to over $1 million in taxes, penalties, and interest owed to the government.

This example illustrates how even a seemingly small mistake can have catastrophic financial repercussions. Therefore, it's essential to thoroughly understand and follow the prohibited transaction rules, especially when using an SDIRA that owns an LLC, as these structures often provide more control, and thus more opportunities for missteps.

What Is a Checkbook LLC?

A checkbook LLC refers to an LLC that is fully owned by an SDIRA and managed by the IRA owner. This structure allows the IRA owner to have direct control over the LLC's bank account, giving them the ability to write checks and make investments without needing to go through the IRA custodian.

The typical process for setting up a checkbook LLC is as follows:

1. The IRA forms an LLC, which is 100 percent owned by the SDIRA.
2. The IRA owner is appointed as the manager of the LLC.
3. The LLC sets up a bank account controlled by the IRA owner/manager.
4. The custodian transfers funds from the IRA into the LLC's account.
5. The IRA owner can now write checks using the LLC's account, giving them full control over the IRA's assets.

While this setup offers flexibility, it also presents significant risks, particularly when it comes to prohibited transactions. Investors who are not thoroughly educated on the rules may unknowingly violate them, leading to severe penalties.

Case Study

NIEMANN V. COMMISSIONER (T.C. MEMO. 2016-11)[53]

In this case, an engineer used a checkbook LLC structure for his IRA investments based on the advice of a promoter. Unfortunately, the operating agreement was poorly customized, and the engineer, unaware of the specific rules, engaged in prohibited transactions with his IRA. As a result, his $230,000 IRA was disqualified, and he faced heavy taxes and penalties. This case serves as a cautionary tale for investors, highlighting the risks of using checkbook LLCs without proper guidance and knowledge.

SWANSON V. COMMISSIONER[54]

The Swanson v. Commissioner (1996) decision is a key case often cited in discussions surrounding IRA-owned LLCs, particularly checkbook LLCs. In this case, Swanson set up a corporation that was entirely owned by his IRA, with himself as the manager. The IRS challenged the structure, arguing that the creation and management of the corporation constituted a prohibited transaction. However, the Tax Court ruled in favor of Swanson, stating that simply setting up the entity and managing it did not violate prohibited transaction rules as long as no disqualified transactions were conducted between the IRA and disqualified persons. This case is frequently used to justify the legality of checkbook LLCs. However, while the Swanson case confirmed that an IRA could own an entity and that the IRA owner could serve as a manager, it did not address many of the complexities involved in managing IRA-owned LLCs. Therefore, investors must be cautious when relying on this case, as it does not provide blanket approval for all types of transactions within an IRA-owned LLC and does not eliminate the risk of prohibited transactions if not carefully managed.

---

[53] Mat Sorensen, "What Not To Do With Your IRA/LLC or Checkbook Control IRA: Niemann v. Commissioner," Directed IRA, December 3, 2020, https://directedira.com/what-not-to-do-with-your-ira-llc-or-checkbook-control-ira-niemann-v-commissioner/.

[54] "Brian D. Swanson v. Commissioner of Internal Revenue, No. 24-11846 (11th Cir. 2024)," Justia, October 4, 2024, https://law.justia.com/cases/federal/appellate-courts/ca11/24-11846/24-11846-2024-10-04.html.

Main Points for Investors Considering IRA-Owned LLCs

While IRA-owned LLCs can be useful in certain situations, they must be approached with caution. The following steps can help ensure that an IRA-owned LLC is structured and managed correctly:

1. Determine necessity: IRA-owned LLCs are not always necessary. Before setting one up, consider whether the benefits outweigh the risks and complexity.
2. Customize the LLC: If an IRA-owned LLC is appropriate, ensure that the operating agreement is fully customized to suit the specific needs of the investor and the investments being made. Avoid using generic templates.
3. Understand the rules: Investors should be well versed in the prohibited transaction rules and how they apply to IRA-owned LLCs. This includes understanding how to avoid common pitfalls such as providing services to the LLC or engaging in transactions with disqualified persons.
4. Consider the costs: You cannot open the IRA-owned LLC personally because your account cannot purchase an asset you own. Therefore, you must have a third party create the special-purpose LLC. Your IRA would then purchase 100 percent of the initial shares. Your account will need to pay the attorney to create this entity. Additionally, states require an annual fee to maintain the LLC status. For example, every LLC in California must pay an annual franchise tax to maintain its active status and good standing, unless it qualifies for an exception. The tax is a flat fee of $800.

When Does an IRA-Owned LLC Make Sense?

There are a few scenarios in which an IRA-owned LLC might be beneficial for investors.

- Asset protection: In high-liability situations, such as holding rental properties, an LLC may offer additional asset protection. However, for low-liability investments, an LLC may not be necessary.
- Quick access to funds: In cases where immediate access to funds is required, such as foreclosure auctions, having control over the LLC's bank account can be an advantage.

- High-volume transactions: For investment strategies involving a high volume of small transactions (e.g., tax lien purchases), an IRA-owned LLC can reduce custodian fees, making it more cost-effective.

Operating Agreement Considerations

A well-drafted operating agreement is essential for an IRA-owned LLC. Some important provisions include:

- Clear purpose: The agreement should clearly state the purpose of the LLC, aligning with IRS guidelines and ensuring that it is designed to protect the IRA's assets.
- Restrictions on services: The IRA owner should avoid providing services to the LLC, such as managing rental properties or coordinating repairs. Instead, third-party managers should be hired to perform these services.
- Non-disqualified manager: To avoid potential prohibited transactions, it may be advisable to appoint a non-disqualified person, such as a trusted friend or property manager, to manage the LLC.

Court Blocks Corporate Transparency Act: LLCs No Longer Need to Register

The Corporate Transparency Act (CTA), which was set to require millions of businesses, including LLCs, to report their owners to the U.S. Treasury Department, has been stopped nationwide by a federal court in Texas. The law was meant to help fight financial crimes like money laundering and terrorism funding by requiring businesses to disclose their owners. However, the court ruled that the law oversteps Congress's authority.

Judge Amos L. Mazzant III ruled that the CTA applies to all incorporated businesses, including those that don't engage in interstate or foreign commerce, which goes beyond what Congress is allowed to regulate under the Constitution. This decision means that LLCs and other businesses no longer need to register their ownership details with the government, as originally required by the CTA.[55]

---

[55] Maureen Leddy, "With Reporting Deadline Looming, Court Blocks Corporate Transparency Act Enforcement," *Thomson Reuters*, December 5, 2024, https://tax.thomsonreuters.com/news/with-reporting-deadline-looming-court-blocks-corporate-transparency-act-enforcement/.

WHAT THIS MEANS FOR BUSINESS OWNERS

The CTA's original deadline required businesses to register their beneficial owners by 2025, but this court ruling puts that requirement on hold indefinitely. Small businesses, including family-owned LLCs, were especially concerned about the extra paperwork and the potential invasion of privacy that the law could bring. The ruling relieves these businesses from having to comply, at least for now.

The government may appeal the decision, but for now, LLCs and other entities can continue operating without the added requirement of reporting their ownership to the Treasury Department. This ruling highlights the ongoing debate over balancing the fight against financial crimes with protecting the rights of business owners.

Trusts vs. LLCs

Some investors are drawn to using trusts instead of LLCs for their IRA-owned entities. However, trusts can be more expensive and complex, often requiring additional scrutiny from tax authorities. In most cases, LLCs offer similar benefits with fewer complications and at a lower cost. Trusts may make sense in certain situations, such as in states where LLCs are prohibitively expensive or where additional privacy is required.

Investors using SDIRAs to invest in real estate or other assets should approach IRA-owned LLCs with caution. While these structures can offer flexibility and asset protection, they also come with significant risks if not properly managed. By working with experienced professionals, customizing the LLC to fit specific needs, and staying informed about the rules governing IRAs, investors can avoid costly mistakes and make the most of their retirement funds.

Chapter 18

Securities Laws: SDIRAs and Solo 401(k) Plans

"Understanding securities laws is critical when investing
with self-directed IRAs and solo 401(k) plans. These laws
are designed to protect investors, but navigating them
improperly can lead to severe penalties and jeopardize your
retirement savings."

—Gene Trowbridge, author of *It's a Whole New Business*

When you choose to open an SDIRA or solo 401(k) plan, you will be able to invest in alternative investments. These types of investments would include real estate owned by limited liability companies (LLCs) or limited partnerships (LPs). Terms used to discuss these investments are "syndications" and "crowdfunding." This way to invest usually involves investing in what is actually a security. In this chapter, we will discuss certain aspects of the securities laws with which you should be familiar.

The Securities Acts of 1933

Purpose of the Law
Because of the amount of money lost in the financial industry crash of 1929, the federal government felt it needed legislation to protect investors. The federal legislation enacted in 1933 is the basis for the security laws we work with today. The securities laws are enforced by the Securities and Exchange Commission (SEC).

The Securities Act of 1933[56] was designed to protect the public from fraudulent investments. It has one basic objective: to require that investors receive financial and other significant information concerning securities offered for sale to the public to allow for informed decisions.

---

[56] *Securities Act of 1933*, GPO: Authenticated U.S. Government Information, accessed September 16, 2024, https://www.govinfo.gov/content/pkg/COMPS-1884/pdf/COMPS-1884.pdf.

Full Disclosure Is Needed for Informed Decisions

A primary means of accomplishing the goal of investors making informed decisions is requiring the full disclosure of important financial information through what is commonly called a private placement memorandum (PPM). It is expected that the information required to be included in the PPM will enable investors to make informed judgments about the units offered in the investment group.

What Is a Security?

The word "security" is defined in the Securities Act of 1933, which includes the term "investment contract," along with many other more familiar terms such as "stock," "bond," or "note."

As it relates to alternative investments involving real estate, it might not be an overstatement to say the intention of Congress was to consider any purchase of real estate a security when it does not involve the direct purchase. When buying real estate as a group purchase, it is a security and it needs to be regulated to protect the public.

The Supreme Court Defines an Investment Contract

In SEC v. W.J. Howey Co., 328 U.S. 293 (1946),[57] the court heard a case involving the sale of parcels of land in a citrus grove to investors over the period of February 1941 to May 1943. The court was asked to rule that the real estate investment plan was actually a security because it was not simply a straight real estate purchase but an investment contract.

The Howey Co. owned large tracts of citrus acreage in Lake County, Florida. For several years, it planted about 500 acres annually, keeping half of the groves for itself and offering the other half to the public to generate cash to help it with the rest of its development. An affiliate Howey-in-the-Hills Service, Inc. was involved in cultivating and developing these groves, including harvesting and marketing the crops.

Each potential investor was offered a land sales contract from the Howey Co. and a service contract from Howey-in-the-Hills, a company that was involved in the actual management of the groves. The investors were told that it was not feasible to invest in the groves without a service contract. Eighty-five percent of the acreage sold

---

[57] "SEC v. W.J. Howey Co., 328 U.S. 293 (1946)," Justia, accessed October 11, 2024, https://supreme.justia.com/cases/federal/us/328/293/#:~:text=For%20purposes%20of%20the%20Securities,whether%20the%20shares%20in%20the.

during a three-year period was covered by service contracts with Howey-in-the-Hills.

When the purchaser chose the service contract from Howey-in-the-Hills, they granted the company a ten-year contract without the option of cancellation. For a specific fee plus the costs of labor and materials, the company was given full discretion and control over the cultivation, the harvest, and the marketing of the crops. All the fruit was pooled and sold, and the investors received an allocation of the net profits.

The business in the citrus grove failed, and investors lost their investments. The investors sued, claiming that what they were sold were unregistered securities in violation of the federal securities laws.

After review, the court felt the facts demonstrated that what on the surface appeared to be simply the sales of individual parcels of real estate to individual investors was actually an investment contract because "…individuals were led to invest money in a common enterprise with the expectation they would earn a profit solely through the efforts of the promoter or of someone other than themselves."[58]

The facts showed the investors had an assumption and expectation of receiving a profit without any active effort on their part. The investors did not expect to use the land themselves but instead were attracted to the investment solely by the prospects of a return on their investment through the efforts of the Howey companies.

An outcome of the Howey case was that the court established a four-prong test (the Howey Test) that has become the basis for determining what constitutes an investment contract under the federal securities laws.

The four factors are:

1. An investment of money
2. In a common enterprise
3. With the expectation of profits
4. Solely through the efforts of the promoter.

Most real estate owned by an investment group managed by the syndicator where there are passive investors would be considered an investment contract.

---

[58] "SEC v. W.J. Howey Co., 328 U.S. 293 (1946)," Justia, accessed October 11, 2024, https://supreme.justia.com/cases/federal/us/328/293/#:~:text=For%20purposes%20of%20the%20Securities,whether%20the%20shares%20in%20the.

Limited Partnerships vs. Limited Liability Companies

The meaning of the word "solely" in the fourth factor of the Howey Test has great importance when discussing whether an interest in a limited partnership or a limited liability company is considered an investment contract.

A limited partner is restricted from any direct role in the management of the group and as such, it is generally agreed that an investment in a limited partnership is an investment in an investment contract. However, a member of an LLC may have the authority and ability to take an active role in management, and further study of the structure of the LLC is needed to make a determination. But most LLCs available for an investment from an SDIRA or solo 401(k) would have an entity or individual who acts as the manager, meeting the meaning of "solely."

PRIVATE PLACEMENT EXEMPTIONS TO THE SECURITIES ACT OF 1933

While the general rule is that all securities offerings must be registered with the SEC, the SEC does not have sufficient manpower to regulate and police every group investment that meets the definition of a security. In addition, it is recognized that many investments that are securities involve small amounts of money and investors who know each other and know the business that is the subject of the investment. As a result, the SEC has established exemptions from full registration for private placements of securities, under Regulation D of the Securities Act of 1933.

REGULATION D OF THE SECURITIES ACT OF 1933 (REG. D)

Reg. D establishes the rules under which a real estate syndicator will likely conduct their group investment business to avail themselves of the need to register their securities with the SEC.

Not Every Investor Needs Protection

The SEC is charged with enforcing the Securities Act of 1933 to protect the public, but as a practical matter, the laws are designed to concentrate on large security offerings offered through the national, public financial markets such as the New York Stock Exchange. The Reg. D exemption will likely cover the majority of the smaller offerings in which IRAs and solo 401(k)s invest.

Accredited Investors Do Not Need Protection

The accredited investor concept was created in 1979 based on categories of investors who can obtain information on which to make an informed decision. Accredited investors, based on objective criteria indicating financial sophistication and ability to fend for themselves, do not require the protections of registration under the federal securities laws. The objective criteria dealt with financial sophistication, net worth, knowledge, experience in financial matters, and the amount of assets under management. Accredited investors are deemed not to need protection as long as they are provided with full disclosure of information needed to be able to make an informed decision.

Accredited Individual Investors

There are eight categories of accredited investors defined in Regulation D, Rule 501 of the Securities Act. The two definitions that are of most importance to investors in alternative investments are:

- Any natural person whose individual net worth, or joint net worth with that person's spouse, exceeds $1 million disregarding the value of the person's primary residence.
- Any natural person who had an individual income in excess of $200,000 in each of the two most recent years or joint income with that person's spouse in excess of $300,000 in each of those years and has a reasonable expectation of reaching the same income level in the current year.

When a syndicator has an SDIRA or solo 401(k) and expresses interest in investing in their offering, the syndicator has two definitions by which they can determine if the entity qualifies as accredited:

- Any entity, with total assets in excess of $5 million, not formed for the specific purpose of acquiring the securities offered, whose purchase is directed by a sophisticated person.
- Any entity in which all of the equity owners are accredited investors. The equity owners may be either individuals or other entities as long as each meet the definition of "accredited."

Nonaccredited Investors Need Protection

Individuals or entities that do not meet the definition of "accredited investors" are classified as "nonaccredited investors." Nonaccredited investors, along with investors who are given inadequate information or are attracted to the investment opportunity through advertising or general solicitation, are deemed to need the protection of the federal securities laws.

THE MOST USED PLACEMENTS EXEMPTIONS AVAILABLE UNDER REG. D

Most sponsors of group investments would like to be exempt from full federal registration. Today, Reg. D includes two rules, Rule 506(b) and Rule 506(c), which makes syndications overwhelmingly exempt from full registration.

Reg. D Rule 506(b): Offerings without regard to dollar amount prohibiting advertising and general solicitation

Under Rule 506, Reg. § 203.506, no maximum dollar amount is established for the offerings and sales of securities. Under the terms of this rule, offerings are exempt from federal registration under the following conditions:

- There may be an unlimited number of accredited investors.
- The number of sophisticated investors shall not exceed thirty-five.
- No general solicitation or general advertising is permitted.

Sophisticated investors are defined in Rule 506(b) as: Each purchaser who is not an accredited investor, either alone or with his purchaser representative(s) has such knowledge and experience in financing and business matters that he is capable of evaluating the merits and risks of the prospective investments, or the issuer reasonably believes immediately prior to making any sale that such purchaser comes within this description.

Recent SEC documents show that 93 percent of all the money raised under the Reg. D exemption is raised under Rule 506(b).

Reg. D Rule 506(c): Offerings without regard to dollar amount permitting the use of advertising and general solicitation

Section 201(a) of the JOBS Act (2012) requires the SEC to eliminate the prohibition on using general solicitation under Rule 506 where all purchasers of the securities are accredited investors and the issuer takes reasonable steps to verify that the purchasers are accredited investors.

The Rule 506(c) exemption is available to the sponsor who wishes to form an investment group raising an unlimited amount of money from an unlimited number of accredited investors. The offering could be a specific, a semi-specific, or a blind pool offering. At the current time, this exemption is only used to raise 7 percent of the money raised under Reg. D.

If you are going to invest in a Rule 506(c) offering, you can expect the syndicator, who needs to take reasonable steps, will ask you to verify that you are an accredited investor by supplying documents such as income tax returns, bank statements, or a letter from your CPA.

Crowdfunding

Title III of the JOBS Act (interestingly entitled the Capital Raising Online While Deterring Fraud and Unethical Non-Disclosure Act of 2012) will allow sponsors to use the internet and social media to raise up to $1 million of securities (adjusted annually for inflation) in a twelve-month period. There is no limit to the number of investors in an offering, but there are limits on the amount of money one investor can invest with a single issuer based on:

- The greater of $2,000 or 5 percent of the investor's annual income or net worth, so long as each such investor's annual income or net worth is less than $100,000, or
- If the investor's annual income or net worth is equal to or more than $100,000, ten percent (10 percent) of the investor's annual income or net worth, not to exceed a maximum aggregate of $100,000 of securities sold.

Any crowdfunding transaction must be conducted using a broker or funding portal, and the issuer of the securities must:

- Disclose the names of directors, officers, and each investor who owns more than 20 percent of the issuer.

- Provide a description of the business and business plan of the issuer.
- Provide income tax returns for the issuer covering the previous year and financial statements of the issuer certified by the principal executive of the issuer; financial statements reviewed by an independent public accountant; or audited financial statements, depending on the amount of the money to be raised in the offering.
- Provide a statement of sources and uses of proceeds.
- Provide other information the SEC prescribes for the protection of the investors.

Additionally, the issuer may not sell the securities themselves outside of the broker or the funding portal and must file annual reports with the SEC.

Plan Asset Rule

The plan asset rule is a misunderstood rule as it relates to investing in alternative investments through LLCs and LPs. The rule provides that assets of a company can be deemed the assets of the retirement plan, and all the laws relating to running a retirement plan must be followed. You can imagine how many laws that will entail.

When 25 percent or more of the ownership of a company is retirement funds, like SDIRAs or solo 401(k)s, the plan asset rule applies. You may have heard some real estate syndicators say that they cannot take more than 25 percent of the funds they are raising into their offering from retirement accounts so that the rule will not apply.

Those syndicators are overlooking one of the several exemptions to the rule. The exemption to the rule is if the LLC or LP meets the definition of a real estate operating company (REOC), meaning that the company is invested 50 percent or more into real estate.

In many real estate offerings, the company owns one asset and, except for some minor amount of working capital, over 50 percent of the company's capital is invested in real estate. In this case, the company is exempt from the rule.

There may be some situations wherein a company has a construction project, but until the property is built, the company does not meet the 50 percent threshold. In that case, the syndicator should consult with an attorney who works with the plan asset rule.

In Closing

When opening an SDIRA or solo 401(k), you'll gain access to a broader range of alternative investments, including real estate held through LLCs or LPs. These investment structures, often referred to as syndications or crowdfunding, typically involve investing in what is classified as a security. Understanding the securities laws, like those from the Securities Act of 1933, is crucial for navigating these investments.

Investors should conduct thorough due diligence when considering investments in LPs, syndications, or other real estate opportunities through an SDIRA. This involves carefully reviewing all investment documents, such as PPMs, to ensure full disclosure and transparency. It's equally important to confirm that any potential investment complies with securities regulations to avoid legal complications. You can find helpful resources to conduct this due diligence from PassivePockets (www.PassivePockets.com).

Seeking guidance from qualified professionals, such as real estate experts, financial advisors, and legal counsel, is essential for navigating the complexities of investing through an SDIRA. By doing comprehensive research and partnering with reputable syndicators and LP managers, you can make informed decisions that align with your financial goals and risk tolerance. Ensuring compliance with securities laws and plan asset rules is crucial to fully leveraging the benefits of these powerful investment tools.

Chapter 19

2024 Developments in IRAs and 401(k)s

"With every new year comes regulatory changes and opportunities for innovation in retirement planning. Understanding the latest developments in IRAs and 401(k) s is essential for maximizing the benefits and ensuring compliance with evolving rules."

—Retirement Industry Trust Association (RITA)

2024 updates to the tax code and the impact of COVID-19 have brought about several new developments, rules, and guidelines for IRAs and 401(k)s. Staying informed about these changes is crucial to managing your investments effectively.

IRA Contribution Limits

Contribution limits for IRAs are updated annually. It's important to check with your tax advisor for the current year's limit based on their specific type of IRA, which could include:

- Traditional IRA
- Roth IRA
- SEP IRA
- SIMPLE IRA
- 401(k), 457, and 403(b)
- Health Savings Account
- Education Savings Account

Recent Developments in IRAs and 401(k)s: Understanding the SECURE Act 1.0 and 2.0

The retirement landscape has seen significant changes over the past few years, primarily driven by legislative updates designed to enhance retirement savings and expand access to retirement accounts. Two key pieces of legislation, the Setting Every Community Up for Retirement Enhancement Act of 2019 (SECURE Act) and the SECURE Act 2.0, of

2022, have introduced substantial modifications to IRAs and 401(k)s. This chapter explores these developments, highlighting how they impact retirement planning and savings strategies.

SECURE Act 1.0: Major Changes

The SECURE Act, signed into law on December 20, 2019, introduced several critical changes to retirement accounts, aiming to increase access to retirement savings and adjust rules to better align with current retirement realities.

ELIMINATION OF AGE LIMIT FOR TRADITIONAL IRA CONTRIBUTIONS

One of the most notable changes made by the SECURE Act was the removal of the age limit for traditional IRA contributions. Previously, individuals over the age of 70½ were not permitted to contribute to a traditional IRA. The SECURE Act changed this rule, allowing anyone with earned income to contribute to a traditional IRA regardless of age. This change enables older workers to continue building their retirement savings.

INCREASE IN REQUIRED MINIMUM DISTRIBUTION (RMD) AGE

The SECURE Act also raised the age for required minimum distributions (RMDs) from 70½ to 72. This adjustment provides retirees with an extended period to allow their retirement accounts to grow tax deferred, thereby potentially enhancing their financial security in retirement.

NEW RULES FOR INHERITED IRAS

Another significant alteration involved the rules governing inherited IRAs. Under the previous regulations, beneficiaries could stretch out distributions over their lifetimes, allowing for prolonged tax-deferred growth. The SECURE Act changed this, generally requiring non-spouse beneficiaries to withdraw the entire balance within ten years of the original account holder's death. Exceptions are made for certain eligible beneficiaries, including spouses, children who are minors, and disabled individuals.

SECURE Act 2.0: Enhancements and New Opportunities

Building on the foundation laid by the SECURE Act, the SECURE Act 2.0 was signed into law by President Biden on December 29, 2022 as part of the Consolidated Appropriations Act, 2023. This legislation further refines retirement savings strategies, aiming to enhance savings and expand access even more.

FURTHER INCREASE IN RMD AGE

One of the key provisions of SECURE Act 2.0 is the increase in the RMD age from 72 to 73, starting January 1, 2023, then to age 75 in 2033. This change provides retirees with additional time to allow their savings to grow before mandatory withdrawals begin, giving them more flexibility in managing their retirement funds.

HIGHER CATCH-UP CONTRIBUTIONS

Catch-up contribution limits are also seeing changes. For 2024 and 2025, the catch-up contribution limits for Traditional and Roth IRAs remain steady at $1,000. Similarly, 401(k) catch-up contributions stay at $7,500 for both years.

The SECURE Act 2.0 introduces a significant provision effective for the 2025 tax year. Active participants aged 60 to 63 can contribute the greater of $10,000 or 150 percent of the indexed 2024 catch-up contribution limit. This provision serves as an amendment to Code Section 414(v). Importantly, just as the age-50 catch-up election is optional, the new age 60-63 catch-up election is also optional.

However, some ambiguity remains. It is unclear whether employers with multiple plans within their controlled group are required to offer the age 60-63 catch-up election universally or if they can implement it selectively on a plan-by-plan basis.

The most notable increase in contributions applies to participants aged 60 to 63, offering them greater opportunities to boost their retirement savings.

EXPANSION OF ROTH CONTRIBUTIONS

The legislation also enhances the ability to make Roth contributions. With SECURE Act 2.0, employers now have the option to match employee contributions with Roth (after-tax) dollars instead of pretax dollars, providing more flexibility in how retirement contributions are managed and taxed.

Additionally, SECURE Act 2.0 allows for the creation of SIMPLE and SEP Roth IRAs starting in 2023. These contributions will be included in the employee's income for the year in which they are made. This change provides more opportunities for tax-free growth and withdrawals in retirement, pending further guidance from the Department of Treasury on implementation.

SUPPORT FOR SMALL BUSINESSES

Recognizing the challenges small businesses face in offering retirement plans, SECURE Act 2.0 introduces measures to simplify plan administration and incentivize plan creation. This includes tax credits to help cover the cost of setting up a retirement plan. For small businesses sponsoring a new defined-contribution plan, the act provides a tax credit for employer-matching contributions, starting at 100 percent for the first two years and gradually decreasing over five years.

The SECURE Act and SECURE Act 2.0 have brought about significant changes to the retirement-planning landscape. By extending the age for required distributions, increasing contribution limits, expanding Roth options, and supporting small businesses, these laws aim to enhance retirement savings opportunities for individuals and promote broader access to retirement plans. Staying informed about these developments is crucial for maximizing your retirement savings and ensuring a secure financial future.

Frequently Asked Questions

Can I sell real estate and become an SDIRA administrator myself?

No. This would be a conflict of interest if you are promoting specific investments or types of investments and could lead to regulatory issues for you and wipe out any IRA investment and tax advantages. The administrator and promoters need to be two separate, independent parties.

Can more than one type of investment be invested in with an SDIRA?

Absolutely. A broad variety of different sectors and assets can be held in a single account. In fact, that's the purpose of enjoying self-directed investing. This includes residential and commercial real estate, mortgage notes, certain precious metals, and qualified private stock.

How long does it take to set up a new SDIRA?

New self-directed retirement accounts can be set up and established in just a day or two. Rolling over existing 401(k)s and IRAs may require ten or more days for funds to be transferred and cleared for investing. Setting up a solo 401(k) can take three to four weeks.

How many U.S. citizens have money in retirement accounts?

Around 42.2 percent of households in the U.S. currently have an IRA.[59] Around 70 million Americans have 401(k)s.

Can U.S. investors use this tool to invest outside the U.S.?

Yes, U.S. investors can use SDIRAs to invest in real estate and other assets outside the United States. Many investors seek to diversify their portfolios by acquiring real estate in countries like Panama, Costa

---

[59] "IRAs Play a Key Role in US Households' Retirement Planning," ICI: Investment Company Institute, February 29, 2024, https://www.ici.org/news-release/24-news-ira-retirement-plan#:~:-text=Washington%2C%20DC%3B%20February%2029%2C,individual%20retirement%20accounts%20(IRAs).

Rica, and Mexico, among others. While this strategy can provide excellent diversification and access to emerging markets, there are important considerations, especially related to the Foreign Bank Account Report (FBAR) rules.

Under the Bank Secrecy Act, investors are required to report certain foreign financial accounts, such as bank accounts, brokerage accounts, and mutual funds, to the U.S. Treasury Department annually. This reporting requirement applies if the aggregate value of the foreign accounts exceeds $10,000 at any time during the year. In addition to filing the FBAR, investors must also maintain records of these accounts.

Investments in foreign real estate, businesses, or other international assets must comply with IRS rules, which prohibit personal use of foreign properties owned by the SDIRA. Additionally, investors should be aware of potential foreign tax obligations and the possibility of double taxation. While tax treaties may offer some relief, it's essential to understand the implications of investing in international markets.

Not all SDIRA custodians allow foreign investments, so it's crucial to ensure your custodian supports these types of transactions. Foreign investments also involve added complexities such as currency exchange risks, higher transaction fees, and navigating different legal environments. As always, thorough due diligence and consultation with qualified tax, legal, and investment professionals are key when considering international investments with an SDIRA.

Why should I incorporate SDIRA investing into my real estate strategy?

As an investor, incorporating SDIRA investing into your real estate strategy can significantly enhance your financial growth. Interest in SDIRAs is rapidly increasing as investors across multiple generations use these accounts to catch up on retirement savings, reduce taxes, and grow their net worth more effectively. With trillions of dollars available in retirement accounts, those who leverage SDIRAs for real estate investments are positioning themselves for long-term success.

By educating yourself on how SDIRAs work and integrating them into your strategy, you not only diversify your portfolio but also take advantage of tax benefits that can accelerate wealth-building. Investors who understand and utilize these tools can create opportunities for higher returns and gain a competitive edge in the real estate market.

Where can I find SDIRA investment opportunities?

To identify SDIRA investment opportunities in real estate, consider reaching out to past connections, tapping into marketing channels, using lead lists, and building relationships with strategic referral partners. Real estate investment clubs and communities are also valuable sources for finding potential deals. By expanding your network and staying informed on SDIRA options, you can unlock new avenues for growth and secure your place in this evolving investment landscape.

Can an SDIRA be opened online?

Yes! Almost all self-directed providers have an online application on their website.

Do you have more questions?

If you want to chat with the BiggerPockets community and tap into their experience, you can visit the forum (www.BiggerPockets.com/Forums51Book).

If you're interested in a passive investing community specifically, check out PassivePockets (www.BiggerPockets.com/PassivePockets). This is an excellent resource for investors looking for investment advice and investment opportunities.

Acknowledgments

As the old saying goes, "No man is an island," nor is any woman. The work it took to create uDirect IRA Services, LLC and this book required more than just one person.

The thanks I owe are too numerous to cover fully in this space. However, I will say that I thank the people who helped me get where I am today as well as those who stood in my way. Both were instrumental in my life's path, and all of my encounters made me stronger, helping me move this book project forward.

First, I would like to thank the BiggerPockets publishing team. They are a powerhouse of organization and execution. Katie, Kaylee, Savannah, and Winsome—you're next level!

In particular, I thank every individual who ever opened an account with uDirect IRA Services. They all receive my gratitude.

To Scott Janko of American Estate & Trust, who believed in my idea when I approached him with the concept of uDirect, thank you! My special thanks also go to Iris Veneration and Bobi Alexander, who helped me find the company's initial equity partners, Wendi Chen and Rose Fruehauf. These powerful women believe in supporting other women in business, which deserves applause. The company now has one owner, but that would not be the case if these women had not provided the gas to get this plane off the ground.

Thank you also to Gene Trowbridge and John Hyre for their collaboration and inspiration—two top-shelf professionals I'm proud to know.

Moreover, where would uDirect be today if not for the much-appreciated dedication of our staff? To Matt Collier, Jon Carino, Kathy Werry, Jeff Dixon, David Rodriguez, Derexa Anstead, Steve Schanke, Tyler Anstead, Mark Gutierrez, Lesly Segura, Khang Nguyen, and others who work on the front lines and who are dedicated to helping our customers, thank you.

Other thanks go to mentors from the past, including Wayne Anthony for his excellent guidance during the Key Club days. Thanks go to Mike Rich, who was probably the best boss I ever had, as well as my mentors, including Paul Aubin, Harry Barth, and Linda Hughes.

Finally, I dedicate this book to my children, Mitchell and Lauren. You are my compelling reasons. Love you!

Glossary of Terms

1031 exchange: A tax-deferral strategy under section 1031 of the Internal Revenue Code (IRC) that allows real estate investors to roll over capital gains into new properties, postponing tax liability until the property is sold without a subsequent exchange.

> *You can learn more about 1031 Exchanges at www.BiggerPockets. com/BookBlog1031Exchange.*

401(k): A tax-advantaged retirement savings account offered by employers, allowing employees to invest part of their paycheck before taxes are taken out.

Acquisition costs: The expenses associated with purchasing an investment, which must be covered by the IRA if it owns the investment.

Adjusted tax basis: The original cost of a property plus improvements, minus depreciation, used to calculate gains or losses for tax purposes.

Appraisal: An evaluation of a property's value, required when withdrawing an IRA-owned property to ensure fair market value is assessed for tax purposes.

Asset allocation: The process of dividing an investment portfolio among different asset categories, such as stocks, bonds, and real estate, to balance risk and reward.

Asset classes: Categories of investments, such as stocks, bonds, real estate, and precious metals, that exhibit similar characteristics and behave similarly in the marketplace.

Broker: A licensed professional who buys and sells assets on behalf of clients, typically charging a commission for their services.

Brokerage: A firm that acts as an intermediary between buyers and sellers to facilitate transactions, often in real estate or finance.

Capital: Financial assets or resources that individuals or businesses use to fund investments, such as purchasing real estate.

Capital gain: The profit earned from the sale of an asset, such as real estate, when the selling price exceeds the original purchase price.

Catch-up contributions: Additional contributions allowed for individuals aged 50 and over, enabling them to contribute more to their retirement accounts beyond the standard limits.

Certified Public Accountant (CPA): A licensed accounting professional who provides financial advice, prepares tax returns, and ensures compliance with tax laws.

You can find an investor-friendly tax professional at www.BiggerPockets.com/BookCPA.

Checkbook control IRA: An SDIRA that is structured as an LLC, allowing the account holder to have direct control over the funds and make investments via a checkbook without needing custodian approval for each transaction.

Closing costs: Fees and expenses incurred during the finalization of a real estate transaction, which must be paid from the IRA when buying property through an SDIRA.

You can learn more about closing costs at www.BiggerPockets.com/BookBlogClosingCosts.

Comingling of funds: The mixing of personal and IRA funds, which is prohibited and can lead to the disqualification of the IRA's tax-advantaged status.

Commercial real estate (CRE): Property used for business purposes, including multifamily apartments, office buildings, retail spaces, and industrial properties, often included in diversified investment portfolios.

> *You can learn more about commercial real estate investing at www.BiggerPockets.com/BookBlogCRE.*

Compliance monitoring: The ongoing process of ensuring that all actions and transactions within an IRA comply with IRS regulations and other relevant laws, a key responsibility of the IRA administrator.

Contribution limits: The maximum amount that can be contributed to a 401(k) plan each year, including both salary deferral and profit-sharing contributions, which varies based on the year and the participant's age.

Custodian approval: The requirement that an IRA custodian reviews and approves transactions to ensure compliance with IRS rules, particularly in complex or high-risk scenarios.

Defined benefit plan: A type of pension plan where the employer guarantees a specific retirement benefit amount based on salary and years of service.

Defined contribution plan: A retirement plan where the employer, employee, or both make contributions on a regular basis, with the final benefit depending on investment performance.

Depreciation (real estate): A tax deduction that accounts for the wear and tear of property over time, allowing investors to reduce their taxable income; particularly beneficial in commercial real estate.

> *You can learn more about real estate depreciation at www.BiggerPockets.com/BookDepreciate.*

Direct investment: An investment in which the investor directly owns the asset, such as real estate or a business, rather than through a pooled fund or partnership.

Disallowed person: Individuals who are prohibited from engaging in certain transactions with an IRA, including the account holder, their spouse, ancestors, descendants, and entities they control.

Disqualified persons: Individuals who cannot engage in transactions with an IRA, including the account holder, their spouse, parents, children, and certain other related parties.

Diversification (real estate): The practice of spreading real estate investments across multiple properties, locations, and property types to reduce risk and increase portfolio stability.

Dollar-cost averaging: An investment strategy where an investor regularly purchases a fixed dollar amount of a particular investment, regardless of its price, reducing the impact of volatility.

Due diligence: The process of thoroughly researching and evaluating an investment or service provider before making a decision.

Earned income: Income from employment or business activities, contrasted with passive income from investments, which is relevant when considering IRA contributions and leverage.

Economic Growth and Tax Relief Reconciliation Act of 2001 (EGTRRA): U.S. tax legislation that introduced significant changes to retirement plans, including the creation of the individual 401(k).

Employer Identification number (EIN): A unique number assigned by the IRS to identify a business entity, required for setting up a solo 401(k) plan, as each plan must have its own EIN.

Estate planning: The process of arranging for the management and disposal of a person's estate during their life and after death, including the use of tools like trusts, wills, and retirement accounts to minimize taxes and maximize asset protection for heirs.

You can learn more about estate planning in Money for Tomorrow: How to Build and Protect Generational Wealth, *by Whitney Elkins-Hutten (www.BiggerPockets.com/ ReadMoneyforTomorrow).*

Ethical standards: The principles and practices that guide the behavior of IRA custodians and administrators, ensuring they act in the best interests of their clients and maintain integrity in their services.

Factoring investments: The purchase of accounts receivable at a discount, allowing businesses to receive cash quickly; can be an investment option in an SDIRA.

Fee structure: The breakdown of fees associated with managing an IRA, including setup fees, annual maintenance fees, transaction fees, and other potential charges, which can impact overall investment returns.

Financial consequences: The positive or negative impact of financial decisions on an individual's or organization's financial health.

Financial future: The anticipated financial status or well-being of an individual or entity based on current savings, investments, and economic factors.

Financial recession: A significant decline in economic activity across the economy that lasts for an extended period, often leading to decreased investment returns.

Financial watchdogs: Organizations or agencies that monitor financial markets and practices to ensure fairness and compliance, such as the SEC, CFPB, and FTC.

Fund manager: A professional responsible for making investment decisions and managing a portfolio of assets within a fund.

Golden years: A term originally referring to peak working and earning years but now commonly used to describe the period of retirement characterized by relaxation and leisure.

Home equity: The market value of a homeowner's unencumbered interest in their property, which can be used as a financial resource in retirement through products like reverse mortgages.

Indirect benefit rules: IRS regulations that prevent individuals from receiving personal benefits from their retirement account investments, which can lead to disqualification and penalties.

Indirect rule: An IRS rule stating that if an action is prohibited directly within an IRA, it is also prohibited indirectly through intermediaries, such as lending money to a relative who then invests in your business.

Individual Retirement Account (IRA): A savings account with tax advantages that individuals can use to save and invest for retirement.

Inherited IRAs: Retirement accounts passed on to beneficiaries after the account holder's death, with specific rules depending on whether the beneficiary is a spouse or non-spouse.

Internal Revenue Code 4975: The section of the tax code that outlines prohibited transactions and the penalties for engaging in them within an IRA.

Internal Revenue Service (IRS): The U.S. government agency responsible for tax collection and enforcement of tax laws.

IRA administrator: A third-party service provider that helps manage the administrative aspects of an IRA, including recordkeeping and compliance with IRS rules, distinct from making investment decisions.

IRA contribution limits: The maximum amount that can be contributed to an IRA each year, varying by account type and the account holder's age.

IRA LLC: An arrangement where an SDIRA owns a limited liability company (LLC), giving the account holder checkbook control over their retirement funds.

Leverage: The use of borrowed capital, such as mortgages or loans, to increase the potential return on investment in real estate, allowing for greater asset control and portfolio growth.

Loan-to-value (LTV) ratio: A financial term that expresses the ratio of a loan to the value of the asset purchased; used by lenders to assess risk.

Luxury single-family rental property: A high-end residential property rented out to tenants, which can be an investment option for an SDIRA.

Marketing budget: The allocated funds used for promoting services, including advertising, direct mail, online campaigns, and events; particularly important for raising awareness about SDIRA and real estate opportunities.

Metals (precious metals): Investments in physical commodities like gold, silver, platinum, and palladium, often used as a hedge against inflation.

Multiple listing service (MLS): A database used by real estate brokers to share information about properties for sale, facilitating collaboration among brokers.

Noncorrelated assets: Investments that do not move in tandem with the broader stock market, often providing diversification benefits.

Nonrecourse loan: A loan where the lender's only recourse in case of default is to seize the collateral (usually the property) without any further claims on the borrower's personal or other assets.

Partnership structure: An arrangement where multiple parties, including an IRA, pool their resources to invest in larger assets, such as real estate, and share in the profits or losses.

> *You can learn more about partnerships in real estate in* Real Estate Partnerships: How to Access More Cash, Acquire Bigger Deals, and Achieve Higher Profits, *by Ashley Kehr and Tony Robinson (www.BiggerPockets.com/ReadPartnerships).*

Passive income: Earnings generated from investments, rental properties, or other ventures in which the individual is not actively involved; often used to supplement retirement income.

Prohibited investments: Investments that cannot be held in an SDIRA, including life insurance, collectibles, and certain types of stock.

Prohibited phrases (advertising): Terms like "guaranteed," "safe and risk-free," or "IRS approved," which should be avoided in marketing to prevent misleading investors and attracting regulatory scrutiny.

Prohibited transaction: Any improper use of an IRA by the account holder, beneficiaries, or disqualified persons, which can lead to severe penalties, including the disqualification of the IRA.

Prohibited transactions: Specific transactions that are not allowed within an IRA, including those that involve self-dealing or benefit disqualified persons, which can lead to severe penalties and disqualification of the IRA.

Protecting Americans from Tax Hikes Act (PATH Act): U.S. legislation that extended and made permanent several tax provisions, including incentives for real estate investments and other economic activities.

Real estate appreciation: The increase in property value over time, contributing to wealth building and offering potential capital gains for real estate investors.

You can learn more about real estate appreciation at www.BiggerPockets.com/BookBlogAppreciation.

Real estate deal: A transaction involving the purchase, sale, or lease of real estate property.

You can look for deals with the BiggerPockets Deal Finder (www.BiggerPockets.com/BookDeals).

Real estate investment: The purchase, ownership, management, rental, or sale of real estate for profit.

Real estate investment trust (REIT): A company that owns, operates, or finances income-producing real estate and allows investors to buy shares in the company, offering a way to invest in real estate without owning the property directly.

Real estate IRA: An SDIRA specifically used to invest in real estate properties, offering tax advantages while diversifying retirement portfolios.

Real estate professional: Individuals involved in various aspects of real estate, including sales agents, brokers, property managers, and real estate consultants.

Real estate retirement accounts: Retirement accounts, including SDIRAs, that allow for the investment of retirement funds into real estate, providing opportunities for tax-advantaged growth and diversification.

REALTOR©: A registered trademark referring to a member of the National Association of Realtors (NAR), who adheres to a specific code of ethics and professional standards.

Refinance debt: Debt incurred when refinancing an existing mortgage, which can also trigger UDFI taxes if the property is owned by an IRA.

Required minimum distribution (RMD): With the advent of the SECURE ACT 2.0, mandatory withdrawals that must begin at age 73 from retirement accounts; designed to deplete the account over the retiree's lifetime.

Rollover: The process of transferring funds from one retirement account to another, such as moving funds from a 401(k) to an SDIRA.

Roth IRA: A type of IRA where contributions are made with after-tax dollars, and qualified withdrawals during retirement are tax free.

Savings incentive match plan for employees (SIMPLE IRA): A retirement plan designed for small businesses and the self-employed, allowing pretax contributions with employer matching.

Self-dealing: A prohibited transaction where the IRA owner engages in activities that benefit themselves or related parties directly or indirectly from the IRA's investments.

Self-directed IRA (SDIRA): A type of individual retirement account (IRA) that allows the account owner to make investment decisions and invest in a wider range of assets than traditional IRAs offer.

Simplified employee pension IRA (SEP IRA): A retirement plan that allows business owners to make significant contributions for themselves and their employees; often used for its higher contribution limits and tax benefits.

Snowball wealth: The concept of gradually growing wealth over time by reinvesting earnings, leading to increasingly larger returns.

S corporation (S corp): A type of corporation that passes income directly to shareholders to avoid double taxation but is generally prohibited from being owned by an IRA.

Social Security Act (1935): A U.S. law signed by President Franklin D. Roosevelt that established a system of old-age benefits for workers, unemployment insurance, and other social welfare programs.

Spousal IRA: An IRA set up for a nonworking spouse, allowing couples to double their retirement contributions, which can be either a traditional or Roth IRA.

Tax advantages: Financial benefits, such as tax deferrals or exemptions, associated with specific investment accounts like IRAs.

Tax attorney: A legal professional specializing in tax law, advising clients on tax-related issues and representing them in disputes with tax authorities.

Tax breaks: Financial advantages that reduce the amount of taxes owed; often associated with retirement accounts and certain types of investments.

Tax-deferred: A status where taxes on investment gains are postponed until the funds are withdrawn; common in traditional IRAs and 401(k)s.

Tax-free income: Income that is not subject to taxes, such as earnings within a Roth IRA, though leveraged income in a Roth IRA may still be subject to UDFI taxes.

Tax liens: A legal claim against property due to unpaid taxes, which can be purchased as an investment, potentially yielding returns if the property owner repays the debt.

Tax professional: A specialist in tax law and preparation who can provide advice on complex financial situations, particularly those involving retirement accounts.

You can find investor-friendly tax professionals at www.Bigger-Pockets.com/BookCPA.

Traditional IRA: A type of IRA where contributions may be tax deductible, and earnings grow tax deferred until withdrawals are made during retirement.

Unrelated business income tax (UBIT): A tax on income generated from business activities unrelated to the IRA's exempt purpose, which can be triggered by certain investments in an IRA.

Unrelated debt-financed income (UDFI): Income derived from debt-financed property in an IRA, subject to taxation under certain conditions.

Volatile stocks: Stocks that experience rapid and unpredictable price changes, leading to higher risk.

Wealth building: The process of generating and accumulating financial assets over time through investments, savings, and other financial strategies.

Peer Reviewed By

Matthew Collier, Operations Manager at uDirect IRA Services

Jeffrey Dixon, VP of Business Development at uDirect IRA Services, LLC

Mary Mohr, Executive Director at RITA

About the Author

Kaaren Hall: CEO of uDirect IRA Services, LLC and the Orange County Real Estate Investors' Association

Kaaren Hall is a financial industry leader with over 20 years of experience in mortgage banking, real estate, and property management. As founder and CEO of uDirect IRA Services, LLC, she has guided the company to manage over $1 billion in assets, helping thousands of Americans diversify their retirement portfolios through SDIRAs.

Kaaren also founded the Orange County Real Estate Investors Association (OCREIA) and serves on the Board of Directors for the Retirement Industry Trust Association (RITA), contributing to the organization's mission of expanding retirement savings opportunities for Americans. Kaaren is recognized for her innovative investment strategies, particularly during challenging economic periods, and her ability to simplify complex financial concepts for investors.

To learn more about Kaaren Hall and her companies, visit uDirect IRA Services LLC (www.udirectira.com) and OCREIA (www.ocreia.com).

Additional Resources

www.investor.gov
(800) 732-0330
The Securities and Exchange Commission (SEC) is dedicated to helping
Americans protect their investments.

www.nasaa.org
(202) 737-0900
The North American Securities Administrators' Association (NASAA)
provides information on investor education.

www.finra.org
(301) 590-6500
The Financial Industry Regulatory Authority (FINRA) has a section
on smart investing.

www.brokercheck.finra.org
Tells you instantly whether a person or firm is registered, as required
by law, to sell securities (stocks, bonds, mutual funds and more), offer
investment advice, or both.

www.aarp.com
(888) 687-2277
American Association of Retired Persons (AARP) includes a section
on scams, fraud, and consumer protection.

www.wikipedia.org
Overview of SDIRAs, allowable and prohibited investments.

www.sec.gov
The U.S. Securities and Exchange Commission regulates businesses
and investments, and provides alerts on fraud issues.

www.census.gov
Deep data on aging, retirement, worker participation, and health from the U.S. Census Bureau.

www.udirectira.com
Detailed information on establishing SDIRA accounts, IRA rules, and a calendar of local events where real estate professionals can learn more about these tools and network with other pros.

www.IRS.gov
Pub 590 describes Traditional and Roth IRA rules. Pub 598 covers UBIT and UDFI taxes.

www.BiggerPockets.com
Join Over 3 Million Real Estate Investors. BiggerPockets brings together education, tools, and a community of more than 3+ million members—all in one place.

www.PassivePockets.com
Access educational resources, private investor forums, and comprehensive sponsor & deal directories — so you can confidently find, vet, and invest in real estate syndications.

Reference List

"401(k) Limit Increases to $23,500 for 2025, IRA limit remains $7,000." Internal Revenue Service. November 1, 2024. https://www.irs.gov/newsroom/401k-limit-increases-to-23500-for-2025-ira-limit-remains-7000.

"5 Hedge Funds Investing in Real Estate in 2024." *The Adviser Magazine*. February 2024. https://theadvisermagazine.com/market-research/investing/5-hedge-funds-investing-in-real-estate-in-2024/.

Basak, Sonali, and Zachary Mider. "Paulson Reinsurer Winds Down After Slump, Tax Criticism." Bloomberg. January 13, 2016. http://www.bloomberg.com/news/articles/2016-01-13/paulson-reinsurer-winds-down-after-slump-bermuda-tax-criticism.

"Brian D. Swanson v. Commissioner of Internal Revenue, No. 24-11846 (11th Cir. 2024)." Justia. October 4, 2024. https://law.justia.com/cases/federal/appellate-courts/ca11/24-11846/24-11846-2024-10-04.html.

Butrica, Barbara, Howard Iams, Karen Smith, and Eric Toder. "The Disappearing Defined Benefit Pension and Its Potential Impact on the Retirement Incomes of Baby Boomers." *Social Security Bulletin* 69, no. 3 (2009), https://www.ssa.gov/policy/docs/ssb/v69n3/v69n3p1.html.

Campbell, Robert, and Lola Panagos. "US Pension Funds Up Real Estate Exposure to Offset Rising Risks." *S&P Global*. August 18, 2022. https://www.spglobal.com/marketintelligence/en/news-insights/latest-news-headlines/us-pension-funds-up-real-estate-exposure-to-offset-rising-risks-71610560.

Caporal, Jack. "Commercial Real Estate Investing Statistics for 2024." *The Motley Fool*. June 28, 2024. https://www.fool.com/research/commercial-real-estate-investing-statistics/.

"Certified Commercial Investment Member (CCIM)." National Associations of Realtors. Accessed November 25, 2024. https://www.nar.realtor/education/designations-and-certifications/certified-commercial-investment-member-ccim.

"Civilian Labor Force Participation Rate." U.S. Bureau of Labor Statistics. Accessed September 16, 2024. https://www.bls.gov/charts/employment-situation/civilian-labor-force-participation-rate.htm.

"Department of Finance Publishes Fiscal Year 2025 Tentative Property Tax Assessment Roll." NYC Department of Finance. January 16, 2024. https://www.nyc.gov/site/finance/about/press/press-release-fy25-tentative-assessment-roll.page.

"Distributions from Individual Retirement Arrangements (IRAs)." Department of Treasury Internal Revenue Service. March 12, 2024. https://www.irs.gov/pub/irs-pdf/p590b.pdf.

"Does Fort Knox Still Have Gold?" Garfield Refining. March 22, 2024. https://www.garfieldrefining.com/resources/blog/does-fort-knox-still-have-gold/.

Ebeling, Ashley. "Tax Hikes Hit Trusts Hard, Beneficiaries Pull Money Out." *Forbes.* January 9, 2013. http://www.forbes.com/sites/ashleaebeling/2013/01/09/tax-hikes-hit-trusts-hard-beneficiaries-pull-money-out/#67471a4b2607.

"Four Facts of Living Trusts." *Kiplinger Personal Finance.* December 31, 2014. http://www.kiplinger.com/article/retirement/T021-C000-S001-four-facts-of-living-trusts.html.

Gandel, Stephen. "America's Biggest Job Market Problem Is Uniquely American." *Fortune.* July 2, 2015. http://fortune.com/2015/07/02/us-labor-force-participation-drops/.

"Global Real Estate Outlook 2024." *JLL.* Accessed September 23, 2024. https://www.us.jll.com/en/trends-and-insights/research/global/global-real-estate-outlook.

Greenhalgh, Hugo. "Low Returns Will Be New Norm for Investors, Say Wealth Managers." *Financial Times.* February 2, 2016. http://www.ft.com/cms/s/0/12df0d5c-c9a3-11e5-a8ef-ea66e967dd44.html#axzz3zblTXln2.

Hart, Jordan. "Mark Zuckerberg Owns Over 1,200 Acres of Land. Here's a Look at His Properties across the US, from a Hawaiian Doomsday Bunker to Lake Tahoe Estates." *Business Insider.* April 7, 2024. https://www.businessinsider.com/inside-mark-zuckerbergs-extensive-real-estate-portfolio-2024-4.

Hayes, Adam. "Protecting Americans from Tax Hikes (PATH) Act: Definition." *Investopedia.* October 24, 2024. https://www.investopedia.com/terms/p/path-act.asp.

Iekel, John. "Retirement: An Historical Perspective." American Society of Pension Professionals & Actuaries. October 4, 2018. https://www.asppa-net.org/news/2018/10/retirement-historical-perspective/.

"IRAs Play a Key Role in US Households' Retirement Planning." ICI: Investment Company Institute. February 29, 2024. https://www.ici.org/news-release/24-news-ira-retirement-plan#:~:text=Washington%2C%20DC%3B%20February%2029%2C,individual%20retirement%20accounts%20(IRAs).

Kennedy, Ellen. "Retirement Savings Calculator: How Much Money Do I Need to Retire?" *Kiplinger Personal Finance.* Updated August 22, 2024. https://www.kiplinger.com/retirement/retirement-planning/600895/retirement-savings-calculator.

"Labor Force Participation Rate." FRED: Federal Reserve Bank of St. Louis. Accessed September 16, 2024. https://fred.stlouisfed.org/series/CIVPART.

Leddy, Maureen. "With Reporting Deadline Looming, Court Blocks Corporate Transparency Act Enforcement." *Thomson Reuters.* December 5, 2024. https://tax.thomsonreuters.com/news/with-reporting-deadline-looming-court-blocks-corporate-transparency-act-enforcement/.

LSARET. "401(k)s Face 'Crisis,' Says Nobel Prize Winner Merton." *Wealth Strategies Journal.* June 25, 2014. https://wealthstrategiesjournal.com/2014/06/25/401ks-face-crisis-says-nobel-prize-winner-merton/.

"Median Sales Price of Houses Sold for the United States." FRED: Federal Reserve Bank of St. Louis. Updated July 24, 2024. https://fred.stlouisfed.org/series/MSPUS.

Merton, Robert C., and Arun Muralidhar. "SeLFIES: A New Pension Bond and Currency for Retirement." Harvard Law School Forum on Corporate Governance. May 20, 2020. https://corpgov.law.harvard.edu/2020/05/20/selfies-a-new-pension-bond-and-currency-for-retirement/.

Mitra, Mallika, Paul Curcio, and David Tony. "How America Saves 2024." *Vanguard.* June 2024. https://corporate.vanguard.com/content/dam/corp/research/pdf/how_america_saves_report_2024.pdf.

Nusbaum, Roger. "Is A Lost Decade for Performance Coming?" *Seeking Alpha.* April 2, 2015. http://seekingalpha.com/article/3048776-is-a-lost-decade-for-performance-coming.

"Release: Quarterly Retirement Market Data." ICI: Investment Company Institute. September 19, 2024. https://www.ici.org/statistical-report/ret_24_q2.

Robbins, Tony. *Money: Master the Game* (Simon & Schuster, 2014).

Rus, Andra. "Top 20 NYC Condo Sales in 2015." PropertyShark. January 13, 2016. http://www.propertyshark.com/Real-Estate-Reports/2016/01/13/top-20-nyc-condo-sales-in-2015/.

Sardana, Sanjeev and Sandeep. "A Compelling Reason To Use Your Roth IRA To Fund Your Startup." *Forbes*. February 22, 2016. https://www.forbes.com/sites/sanjeevsardana/2016/02/22/compelling-reason-to-use-your-roth-ira-to-fund-your-startup/.

"Saver's Credit Can Help Low- and Moderate-Income Taxpayers to Save More in 2024." IRS: Internal Revenue Service. November 22, 2023. https://www.irs.gov/newsroom/savers-credit-can-help-low-and-moderate-income-taxpayers-to-save-more-in-2024.

"SEC v. W.J. Howey Co., 328 U.S. 293 (1946)." Justia. Acessed October 11, 2024. https://supreme.justia.com/cases/federal/us/328/293/#:~:text=For%20purposes%20of%20the%20Securities,whether%20the%20shares%20in%20the.

Securities Act of 1933. GPO: Authenticated U.S. Government Information. Accessed September 16, 2024. https://www.govinfo.gov/content/pkg/COMPS-1884/pdf/COMPS-1884.pdf.

Short, Joanna. "Economic History of Retirement in the United States." Economic History Association. Accessed September 16, 2024. https://eh.net/encyclopedia/economic-history-of-retirement-in-the-united-states/.

"Single-Family Rent Growth Tripled Year Over Year in December, CoreLogic Reports." CoreLogic. February 15, 2022. https://www.corelogic.com/press-releases/single-family-rent-growth-tripled-year-over-year-in-december-corelogic-reports/.

Sorensen, Mat. "What Not To Do With Your IRA/LLC or Checkbook Control IRA: Niemann v. Commissioner." Directed IRA. December 3, 2020. https://directedira.com/what-not-to-do-with-your-ira-llc-or-checkbook-control-ira-niemann-v-commissioner/.

Sortino, Frank, and Hal Forsey. "Everyone Is Focusing on the Wrong Goal in Retirement Planning." *Pensions & Investments*. November 24, 2014. http://www.pionline.com/article/20141124/PRINT/311249997/everyone-is-focusing-on-the-wrong-goal-in-retirement-planning.

Spector, Nicole. "Suze Orman: 'How Much Do I Need to Retire?' Is a Stupid Question! Here's How to Save." *Today*. September 25, 2015. https://www.today.com/money/suze-orman-how-much-do-i-need-re-tire-stupid-question-t45051.

"Tax Exempt Bonds Private Letter Rulings: Some Basic Concepts." IRS: Internal Revenue Service. Accessed September 16, 2024. https://www.irs.gov/tax-exempt-bonds/teb-private-letter-ruling-some-basic-con-cepts#:~:text=A% 20private%20letter%20ruling%2C% 20or,taxpay-ers%20or%20by%20IRS%20personnel.

"The National Debt Is Now More Than $35 Trillion. What Does That Mean?" Peter G. Peterson Foundation. July 29, 2024. https://www.pgpf.org/infographic/the-national-debt-is-now-more-than-35-trillion-what-does-that-mean.

Tostevin, Paul, and Charlotte Rushton. "Total Value of Global Real Estate: Property Remains the World's Biggest Store of Wealth." *Savills*. September 2023. https://www.savills.com/impacts/market-trends/the-total-val-ue-of-global-real-estate-property-remains-the-worlds-biggest-store-of-wealth.html.

U.S. Census Bureau. "Mortgage Status." *American Community Survey, ACS 5-Year Estimates Detailed Tables, Table B25081*. 2022. https://data.census.gov/table/ACSDT5Y2022.B25081.

"U.S. Regulators Tackle Money Laundering in the Luxury Home Market." *Thomson Reuters*. Accessed September 16, 2024. https://legal.thomson-reuters.com/en/insights/articles/u-s-regulators-tackle-money-launder-ing-luxury-home-market.

U.S. Retirement Assets: Data in Brief. Congressional Research Service. September 20, 2023. https://crsreports.congress.gov/product/pdf/R/R47699.

"Ultimate Guide to Retirement: What Is a SIMPLE IRA." *CNN Money*. Accessed September 16, 2024. https://money.cnn.com/retirement/guide/IRA_SIMPLE.moneymag/index.htm.

"Understand Market Behavior: Research and Statistics." NAR: National Association of Realtors. Accessed September 23, 2024. https://www.nar.realtor/research-and-statistics.

Wang, Penelope. "This Nobel Economist Nails What's Really Wrong with Your 401(k)." Money.com. June 29, 2014. https://money.com/this-nobel-economist-nails-whats-really-wrong-with-your-401k/.

BiggerPockets®

BiggerPockets "Tax, Self-Directed IRAs and Cost Segregation Forum"
www.BiggerPockets.com/Forums51Book

BiggerPockets Money podcast
"IRA vs. 401(k): Which is the Best Retirement Account for Beginners?"
www.BiggerPockets.com/BookIRAvs401k

BiggerPockets Real Estate podcast
www.BiggerPockets.com/BookRealEstatePodcast

BiggerPockets blog - Personal Finance category
www.BiggerPockets.com/BookBlogPersonalFinance

The Book on Tax Strategies for the Savvy Real Estate Investor
www.BiggerPockets.com/ReadTaxSavvy

The Book on Advanced Tax Strategies: Cracking the Code for Savvy Real Estate Investors
www.BiggerPockets.com/ReadAdvancedTax

Tax Professional Finder
www.BiggerPockets.com/BookCPA

Resource Hub - Financing and Taxes category
www.BiggerPockets.com/BookFinancingAndTax

PassivePockets ®

LEARN HOW TO FIND, VET, AND INVEST IN REAL ESTATE SYNDICATIONS.

PassivePockets is the go-to resource for passive investors seeking to make more informed investment decisions.

OUR PLATFORM OFFERS

EDUCATIONAL RESOURCES

Masterclasses, articles, podcasts, and a weekly newsletter—all designed to give you the edge.

DUE DILIGENCE TOOLS

Rigorous vetting frameworks and community-sourced sponsor ratings & reviews.

INVESTOR-ONLY SPACES

Private forums and weekly Zooms, exclusive to investors—no sponsors or capital raisers allowed.

SPONSOR DIRECTORIES

Detailed profiles with track records, investor reviews, strategies, and more.

DEAL DIRECTORIES

Comprehensive deal profiles, webinars, and direct sponsor connections in dedicated forums.

RATINGS & REVIEWS

Honest feedback from members who have invested with sponsors— the good, the bad, and everything in between.

Our mission is clear: To shine a light on the passive investing space and provide you with the tools and knowledge to navigate it more confidently. PassivePockets is designed to do just that.

PassivePockets.com

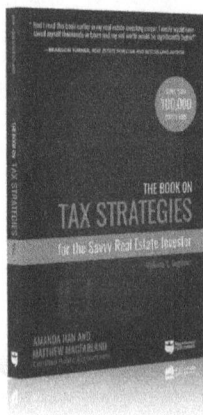

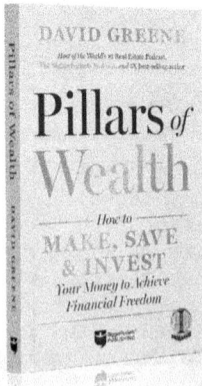

Looking for more?
Join the BiggerPockets Community

BiggerPockets brings together education, tools, and a community of more than 2+ million like-minded members—all in one place. Learn about investment strategies, analyze properties, connect with investor-friendly agents, and more.

Go to **biggerpockets.com** to learn more!

Listen to a **BiggerPockets Podcast**

Watch **BiggerPockets on YouTube**

Join the **Community Forum**

Learn more on **the Blog**

Read more **BiggerPockets Books**

Learn about our **Real Estate Investing Bootcamps**

Connect with an **Investor-Friendly Real Estate Agent**

Go Pro! Start, scale, and manage your portfolio with your **Pro Membership**

Follow us on social media!

Join over 3 million investors on BiggerPockets forums. Whether you're a seasoned expert or just starting out, tap into the collective knowledge, confidence, and connections to reach your full potential.

Join the conversation now!
BiggerPockets.com/BookForums

BiggerPockets®

www.ingramcontent.com/pod-product-compliance
Lightning Source LLC
Chambersburg PA
CBHW071548200326
41519CB00021BB/6654